THIS IS HOW I SPEAK

THIS IS HOW I SPEAK

THE DIARY OF A YOUNG WOMAN

SANDI SONNENFELD

IMPASSIO PRESS
SEATTLE

Cover Photo: University of Washington/Mary Levin
Author Photo: Warren Berry
Design: Phil Kovacevich/Kovacevich Design

Portions of this book were first published in the
anthology *Darkness and Light: Private Writing as Art*,
edited by Olivia Dresher and Victor Muñoz.

First Printing – 2002

Impassio Press is a small literary press devoted to
publishing a variety of fragmentary writings, with a
focus on journals, diaries, and notebooks.

Library of Congress Control Number: 2002101354

ISBN: 0-9711583-1-2

Impassio Press, LLC
P.O. Box 31905
Seattle, WA 98103
www.impassio.com

CONTENTS

ACKNOWLEDGEMENTS

Writing may be a solitary art, but perhaps more than anything else I have composed, this manuscript demonstrates just how important outside influences are in shaping who and what we are. As such, I feel that I must acknowledge several people who played a role in helping to develop this book.

A heartfelt thanks to Miguel Scherer and Phyllis Hatfield, who offered me great insights about the manuscript and the publishing process. Thanks also to my editor and publisher, Olivia Dresher, for immediately understanding what this book was meant to be.

My deepest appreciation to Regina Maruca, Emily Economou, Marg Stark, Kathi Morrison, Jeanie Murphy, and Linda Dunjacik, who not only often serve as my first readers but, despite the geographic distances that separate us, have generously given me their unfailing friendship, love, and support.

And finally, to my husband, Warren Berry, for being there every day.

PREFACE

This Is How I Speak is directly based on the journal I kept during my first year in the MFA program in Creative Writing at the University of Washington in Seattle. Traditional memoirs too often result in a re-writing of events either due to memory lapses, or to make the narrative more dramatic, or in the attempt to make the author appear more sympathetic or intelligent in the face of adversity. Perhaps that's why, in the ten years or so since I first wrote these journal entries, both agents and publishers alike have tried to convince me to turn the manuscript either into a novel or a memoir. Looking back on these pages now, just as all of us look back on our youth, I sometimes ask myself if I should have done things differently or simply taken myself less seriously. And the answer is "of course." But that is the very nature of aging; we gain wisdom with experience, and we ultimately learn that those things which felt so painful in our early twenties become of little consequence in our thirties and forties.

In certain entries, to make the narrative flow more effectively or because I felt readers needed more background to understand the issues I was speaking about, I cut or added additional text. To protect the privacy of the people mentioned in the journal, since I am sure they never knew I was writing about them or that some day that writing might result in publication, I changed names or merged identities. But apart from those minor changes, I deliberately chose to leave the entries as they were when I first wrote them, because to alter them would be to denigrate the thoughts and feelings of a twenty-four-year-old American woman artist struggling to make sense of herself in a world that largely neither admires artists nor women.

I am grateful to Olivia Dresher of Impassio Press, the publisher of this book, who instinctively understood my intent, even when other editors did not. This book simply tries to capture a year in time—a time of both pain and growth, a time of great despair and great happiness—in short, a year in the life of a human being on the threshold of adulthood.

THIS IS HOW I SPEAK

Autumn

Many women writers, learning of Anne Sexton's death, have been trying to reconcile our feelings about her, her poetry, her suicide at forty–five, with the lives we are trying to stay alive in.... But because of her work she is still a presence; and as Tillie Olsen has said: "Every woman who writes is a survivor."

—Adrienne Rich, "Anne Sexton: 1928–1974"
from *On Lies, Secrets, and Silence*

.

I know all about fear. I fear dogs, horses, sharks, snakes, most seafood, farts, hairy men, earthquakes, hurricanes, and flash floods. Basically, anything that can sneak up and surprise me. I'm afraid of failure, growing old, gaining weight, the whole concept of motherhood, and insurance salesmen. But most of all, I'm terrified of complacency, the fear that I might settle for what I have simply because I'm afraid of so much else. I know that I have reached that moment when I get a terrifying feeling that my insides have been bleached white, parched and dry and empty of all ideas.

I am driven by the image of bleached white bones and a growing sense of my becoming ordinary, something more intolerable than all the sharks, dogs, and earthquakes put together.

This is why, despite everything, I am now flying three thousand miles west in a 747 jet en route to Seattle to begin the MFA program in Creative Writing at the University of Washington.

In Boston, I have left behind a love for the city's old historic walkways, a secure though rather unchallenging job as an editorial assistant for a textbook publishing house, my best friend Rachel, my nightly ballet class at a small professional studio in Copley Square, and my Harvard-trained psychotherapist.

In the cargo hold of the plane, I have two suitcases of clothes, eight leotards, three pairs of worn *pointe* shoes, a $2,000 check from my dead grandmother, a three-hundred-page manuscript that represents my first novel, and six books: Margaret Atwood's *Bodily Harm*, Joan Didion's *Democracy*, *The Complete Stories of F. Scott Fitzgerald*, John Fowles's *The Magus*, painter Ben Shahn's *The Shape of Content*, and Helen Lefkowitz's *Alma Mater*, which recounts the establishment of Mount Holyoke College, my undergraduate institution and perhaps the place which up to now has had the biggest impact on my life.

Out of all the hundreds of other books I left behind at my parents' house on Long Island, where I grew up, I chose these six books because I hope they will serve as talismans against evil and mediocrity.

Too often evil and mediocrity go hand-in-hand, like the time back in high school when two of my classmates broke into my locker and stole my awards jacket which I had received for dance achievement at my local ballet studio. When I confronted the two girls and demanded my jacket back, one punched me hard in the right arm. Then, as I watched in horror, the second girl lit up a cigarette and deliberately burned a hole through one of the award badges sewn onto the nylon lining of the jacket.

"That will teach you to think you are better than us," the girl said, and tossed the jacket onto the dirty hallway floor.

I wish I could say that I hurled curses at the girls, the sort of curses that witches unleash on their enemies in bad horror novels—electric death rays, impalement on the sharp ivory husks of a mad elephant, permanent disfigurement by a green and purple skin fungus—but everything happened so fast, the painful throbbing of my bruised arm, the rotten smell of the cigarette burning through the material of my jacket, that my mind snapped shut like a trap, leaving me completely wordless.

And the girls had been right. I didn't think that I was better than them because I could dance, but because I knew that I had within me the power to create while they only had the power to destroy the creations of others. But when I failed to summon up the words from inside of me, I realized suddenly how fleeting the power of creation really is. Without warning, it can disappear (dare I say it?) in a puff of smoke.

Which is perhaps why I now always carry a small, cloth-bound journal in which to record my thoughts. And as I write now, the stale air in the plane's cabin blows down upon me, permeating my clothes. The pilot announces that just below us is Mount St. Helens, which blew its top in 1980. Many of the passengers crane their necks trying to look out the tiny, blunted windows of the plane. I'm seated in the aisle, so when I look over all I see is blinding sunlight.

In elementary school, we always studied volcanoes right before we studied dinosaurs, so I think for a long time I was under the illusion that, like those gigantic animals, volcanoes were extinct. I mean, I saw *Fantasia* a lot as a kid—"The Night on Bald Mountain" scene, where the world is created and then the dinosaurs and the volcanoes fall prey to the Ice Age. Anyway, this is what I think of when the pilot mentions St. Helens—cartoon lava covering the earth. But now I'm going to reside in the presence of not one active volcano but two. (The university brochure says St. Helens's twin, Mount Rainier, is visible from nearly all the buildings on campus.)

I try to decide whether to add erupting volcanoes to my list of fears.

Still, I can understand why a mountain may occasionally need to blow its top. Perhaps it fears complacency as much as I do—decides to stir up the wildlife and human fauna a bit to remind them not to take its existence for granted.

"I am here," the mountain says, feeling a deep stirring somewhere within its fiery belly. "This is how I speak."

SEPTEMBER 14

After a few frantic days of unpacking my bags, settling into graduate housing (I'm living with three other women—all of whom seem nice enough, though somewhat remote), finding a part-time job as an editorial assistant at the University Extension Office and registering for courses, I finally have the chance to go see Daria George, my former dance advisor at Mount Holyoke, who currently chairs the University of Washington Dance Department.

I tell myself that I am really just going to drop by her office to gain my entry card so that I can register for the advanced-level ballet class. Yet, while I dress, making sure of course to wear my ever-slimming black leggings and oversized T-shirt, my hands begin to shake. I look at my hair in the full-length mirror. Shall I wear it down or in a ponytail?

The ponytail makes me look younger, vulnerable, but then I always worry about the small wisps of hair that gather at the top and sides of my forehead, messy annoying curls that no matter how much gel I use never stay in place.

And Daria's walnut-colored eyes notice everything, can tell in a second if a dancer's pelvis is tilted forward even the slightest bit (thus ruining the body's alignment) even when covered by a leotard and baggy sweatpants.

After two years, I am going to see Daria again. I am going to see the only person I know from home, the person whom I most want to be like.

Still in my stocking feet, I do a *tendu* before my full-length mirror, checking to see if all the foot work I did with Nicole in Boston has indeed made my arches more curved, strengthened the shape of my *pointe*.

I think about Nicole—Nicole, who on the first day I arrived at her Boston studio, said to me, "Somebody told you that your feet were the wrong shape to dance. But I can make them better. I can make you beautiful."

For four years I struggled at Mount Holyoke to get such a hopeful prognosis from Daria, for Daria to even acknowledge that there were qualities in my dancing that were worthwhile. For four years I struggled and then suddenly in a single day in Boston, Nicole promised to help me. And she did, which is perhaps why I now have the courage to face Daria again. I want her to look at my feet and see all the work I've done. To look at my feet and realize that she is wrong about me. I have the ability. I have enough talent to dance for her upon the stage.

Daria was the one who put the idea of Seattle in my head. She grew up here and used to tell me how Seattle's artistic community was about to explode on the national scene, but that the city was still small enough for someone to make her mark.

And when she sent me a letter telling me of her new position, I immediately submitted my graduate school application to the UW. Even as I wrote my admissions essay, talking about my great need to pursue my writing, I knew that my real great need was to be with Daria again, to show her how much my dancing had improved.

So now I'm doing it. I climb the three flights of stairs of Meany Hall to the studios. I knock on her office door. The door opens. I scan her features hungrily, trying to see what impact time has made on her wonderful face, her slightly beaked nose, the high cheekbones, both a throwback to her grandmother's Cherokee ancestry. Even when working in her office, she is always dressed in dance clothes, a soft blue sweater over her faded gray unitard and short black skirt. The unitard stops right below her perfectly shaped calves. The lower part of her legs and ankles are bare. On her feet, no socks but a worn pair of black jazz shoes that mold to her strong, highly arched feet like a second skin.

Daria does not know this, but the year I graduated from Mount Holyoke, a photographer friend of mine gave me a picture of Daria that he had taken when she played Ariel in a college production of *The Tempest*. The picture was taken years before I had ever met her, but that photograph captured her in the way that I always thought of her in my head, an elfin being, elusive and open at the same time, an enchanting combination that makes me itch with longing.

"It's me," I say to her now. "I'm here."

She stares at me a moment, then embraces me in a warm hug.

I breathe in the smell of her, hoping that maybe some of her talent will be absorbed by my skin.

"She loves me," I tell myself. "I know she loves me. Why, oh why, is that not enough?"

I am determined to prove myself.

In our last session together, my therapist, Gloria, told me that after a ten-year hiatus from painting, she was having a showing of her work in a Cambridge gallery. One of the pieces that would be displayed was a picture of me—"Dancer at Her Typewriter" is what she calls it.

"You painted a picture of me?" I ask, moved.

"We have seen each other once a week for the past eighteen months," she says. "You sit across from me and we talk. Your features are pretty well burned into my brain."

"Do you paint all your patients?" I ask, suddenly envisioning myself hung between pictures of an obsessive-compulsive and a schizophrenic *(Step right up, ladies and gentlemen, and don't miss this classic portrait of a neurotic in action).*

"No," she says. "In fact, I don't usually do people—mostly abstracts. But your dedication to your art has moved me. We're an awful lot alike."

"We are?" I say, instantly depressed, realizing that for eighteen months I had been talking to a woman who, under different circumstances, could perhaps have been a friend. Alone in bed at night, I never speculated about what Gloria's life was like outside the office—she seemed so together to me, so confident and precise; she made me feel better about myself and for this I was grateful to her. I was also resentful that I couldn't manage to hold my life together without her, that I had to pay her $60 an hour so that I could feel better about myself.

But now, she has painted a picture of me—a portrait to be hung for all of greater Boston to see. I received a photograph of the picture today in the mail, a picture of it hanging in the gallery. And it does look like me, in a way. The curly wild hair tumbling down over bare shoulders, eyes downcast like blank half-moons, pale bluish skin. She put me in a pink tutu, something I've never worn, and I sit with one leg stretched out and one leg tugged up under me, looking down at an old portable Smith-Corona.

I recognize the pose. It's how I used to sit in Gloria's office on those particularly hard days of therapy, on the days when I needed my flesh near me, around me, to remind me that I was real.

Dancer at Her Typewriter.

A dancer who pounds out her feelings on the page, because she has never quite been able to convey them on the stage.

A dancer who became a writer simply because she failed at dancing and a college professor once said that she wrote very well.

I am touched; I am honored. I am twenty-four years old and a portrait of me hangs in a gallery. It is the sort of thing I used to fantasize about when I was eight years old—being famous, being known, being loved, though in my childhood fantasies it was always a man who discovered me, a great man who recognized my talent and introduced me to the world.

Instead it is my female shrink who painted me, my shrink whom I sought out in part because none of those childhood fantasies had come true and I was finding it difficult to accept.

I stare at the picture and feel myself a fraud, a quasi artist, caught between two desires and therefore unable to have either one.

SEPTEMBER 17

Today, in my first writing workshop, the instructor, Camden Dearborn, asked the class to write a creed, a sort of motto that we carry with us about what we expect from writing, etc.

My first reaction is one of frustration. I want to learn how to become a better writer, not discuss why I do it. Why one writes doesn't matter; only THAT YOU WRITE.

As for my expectations, I expect everything from myself and the only thing I expect from publishers, agents, editors, etc., is that they be fair, that they acknowledge and recognize what is good, that artistic merit and marketability be not oxymoronic terms.

So I've been sitting here at my desk, racking my brain trying to come up with something I can say that doesn't come across as a giant caricature, false platitudes about the nobility of writing.

A creed. A motto. All I can think of is the motto from *The Three Musketeers*—one for all, all for one—but that has absolutely no relevance to the solitary, secretive act of writing.

No, maybe my creed is more like Robin Hood's, you know the guy, not the Errol Flynn type, but the one Disney showed us, a dapper brown fox, dressed in green feathers and cap, who stole from the rich and gave to the poor... He *has* to steal, that is what foxes do, but he is a complex little animal, fully equipped with an inflated sense of importance and a sneaking suspicion that any moment now a bigger animal may come blazing out of Sherwood Forest and take away whatever he has worked so hard to get. So he does what any fear-ridden fox would do: He fakes confidence, pulls back his bow, and launches his arrow into the cartoon wind. If his aim is true, he will share the spoils with others.

Writing is like that, stealing life experiences and people met, and with a little bit of juggling, turning it into fiction, giving it back to the Life that so grudgingly bore it. And in the process, a little gold comes into my hands, rarely in the form of currency, but in comprehension. Comprehension of those experiences that before made little sense, and the comprehension that comprehension itself doesn't really matter. What does matter is that comprehension is an act of movement, and therefore through writing, I can go places even when all other action has stopped.

One must act craftily, of course, be expert at robbing images, repeating sounds, colors, and despair, along with the bravado to say, like Robin Hood, "Yep, it's my work. I did it. What are you going to do about it? Publish it?"

And if one is expert enough, there is freedom to take a few more risks, each a little more daring. Every time I start a new piece of writing, it is the second hardest thing I've ever done. Staying alive in the forest is the first.

I had an idea for a story tonight, staring in the mirror that I stare into every night, checking to see if during the day the body has turned perfect, if the legs have grown long and the ankles stronger.

I thought suddenly what it would be like to have a silent character in a story, a woman completely silent, forever staring at the mirror, and how readers would come to know her from the voices of others—her mother, her brother, her first lover, her doctor—for she is only mute because all the other voices have taken hold of her.

I am not being at all clear about the idea of the story. In my mind, I keep calling her "Beauty," but that would be far too allegorical and contrived.

But I know about voices that catch hold of you, stick to you like an overeager cop shadowing a suspected criminal. When I was a little girl, my father once caught me staring in a full-length mirror like the one I have now. I stared at the looking glass, fascinated by the odd shapes my facial features took on simply by flexing or tensing my mouth and jaw muscles.

"What are you doing?" my father said.

I turned towards him still in mid-pose, my tongue poking a fleshy hill in my left cheek, my nose pointing towards the right.

I waited for him to laugh.

"Nice girls shouldn't stare at themselves in mirrors," my father said. "It makes them vain."

His words stung, especially since it was uncharacteristic of my father not to approve of nearly everything his children did. While other parents hung their kids' colored drawings and papers on the refrigerator door with a magnet, my father called my grandmother on the phone and read one of our essays to her aloud, laughing in delight whenever he came across a certain phrase that especially pleased him.

I wanted more than anything to please my father, and the idea that he no longer thought I was "nice" upset me greatly.

"Sugar and spice and everything nice, that's what little girls are made of," the old nursery rhyme played in my head.

"Now play nice with each other," my father would always admonish us kids if we began fighting over where a particular wooden block would go to complete our miniature city that we were building underneath the Ping-Pong table.

But how does one go about being "nice"? Even at eight, I dreamed of being glamorous and smart, like Barbara Stanwick or Katherine Hepburn in the old RKO movies, women who with a single scathing look can silence even the most difficult man but somehow or other still wind up getting kissed by him.

When my older sister would bring home a sick bird or wounded animal to nurse back to health, my mother would reluctantly find a place in the basement to set up a tiny hospital for my sister to administer to her patients. She did so reluctantly, fearing a messy house and animal germs, but I also could see pride in my mother's face that my sister had so much compassion for others.

Frankly, the thought of tending to anything broken or bleeding made me ill, and I always avoided the basement when my sister was on sick duty. Besides, nurses wore boring white uniforms and ugly crepe-soled shoes and smiled benevolently like Florence Nightingale did in her picture in my fourth-grade history book. "The Lady with the Lamp," the soldiers of the Crimea called her.

To hell with benevolence, I wanted to have the lamp, the lime-light, shine down on me, not carry it to shine on others.

Then, in college, I read in an etymology book that the word "nice" originally meant "to be ignorant, to not know." No wonder that society for the past thousand years has encouraged girls to be "nice." Nice girls don't cause trouble for the state; they make no demands, for they are unaware of all that they are missing out on.

So now I view my nightly ritual before the mirror as my form of rebellion against my father and the world. I get guilty pleasure from it; for two or three minutes each night, I glory in the fact that I know my body intimately, something that only I can own.

Nonetheless, my father's admonishment still lingers inside me, a niggling reminder of something that I've failed to do. It remains there on my "to do" list for later in life, after I am famous and successful, when I am old and my body no longer will matter so much. At the top of the list is "Be nice," followed by "Learn how to balance my checkbook," "Study Italian," and "Help save the world."

OCTOBER 1

I am standing in line in ballet at the back corner of the studio, waiting for my turn to perform the *grande allegro* on the floor. The piano thumps out the same tune over and over, a big crashing note on beats one and eight to help us know when to leap.

About fifteen of us are clumped against the wall, so when one of the male dancers speaks, at first I'm not sure it is to *me*.

"You are so in control," he says. "And have really high extensions."

I look at the guy carefully, a man only in his twenties and yet already beginning to go bald, a long, skinny body, but lovely, lovely feet. I crave his feet, their wide spread that easily absorbs the impact when he lands his jumps, his nicely bowed arches that when he points his toes creates a near perfect line.

Dancers are the only people I know who look at a person's feet to measure one's worth. Audiences don't gasp at the beauty of a dancer's face; with the stage so far away, one can just barely make out a dancer's features—no, it is line that they marvel over, that long fluid line that runs from the top of a dancer's head all the way down to the tip of her toes. It is line and the seeming effortlessness with which a dancer executes every step.

I used to adore summers back in New York, not only because I commuted into Manhattan to take dance class every day, but because in the summer women wore sandals, which gave me a nearly unobstructed view of their feet. I would walk down Seventh Avenue, heading towards the 59th Street studio, and evaluate the anklebones, arches, and metatarsals of the women as they walked by.

My best friend, Rachel, once observed that no matter what men might think, women never dress for the men in their lives—they dress for other women—a foolish but deadly serious form of competition. And in the dance world, where there is only one company position for every two hundred ballerinas who apply, I check out other women's feet out of fear and jealousy. Any minute another woman might round the corner with higher arches than mine, a stronger *pointe*.

Because even though I know that I do have high extensions, that when I do an *arabesque* or *dévelopé* my leg does go up, I also know that my arches are too low and my feet too narrow and that there isn't a thing I can do about it.

And here this guy thinks I'm so in control…

"Thank you," I say to the guy who has just complimented my dancing. "Thank you very much."

And then on the count of one I gather my body under myself and with the smallest of breaths, I launch myself onto the dance floor.

Daria yells at me as I execute the sequence.

"Break out," she says, her voice rising above the music. "Break out. Show me that you love to dance."

I try to show her. Year after year after year.

But the fear that I'm second best always gets in the way.

OCTOBER 20

Today I auditioned for the faculty dance concert to be held this winter. I know that I shouldn't have done it. I'm supposed to be out here to become a better writer, to learn to move in that world, yet I couldn't resist. I couldn't resist the opportunity to dance for Daria.

"Don't do it for me," Daria once told me, long ago. "Don't worry about whether or not I will like it, dance for yourself."

And even longer ago, I did it for myself. When I was ten years old, movement was the most important thing in my life. I would dance in the shower, my bedroom, our long narrow kitchen with the linoleum floor. I would even dance in the car, while my mother drove me to ballet class, moving my arms through second position, third, fifth arabesque.

"Stop it," my mother would say. "Stop moving around in the seat; I can't see the cars next to me."

So I would hold still for a second, a rest, a definite pause, but even that was movement, for I could feel the stillness inside me, growing into a burst of energy so intense that at last it had to seek release through my toes. I began to tap my feet to a beat in my head.

My mother sighed.

And when I would finally arrive at class, I would look at myself in the endless row of mirrors and dream about the time when I would be older, fifteen or sixteen, old enough to apprentice to a company, my body long and muscular without a trace of fat or weakness. I would be sleek as a cat, beautiful, untouchable like the girls I saw at American Ballet Theatre or City Ballet, performing Giselle, the Black Swan, the Sugar Plum Fairy.

I dreamed so hard and so long that when I finally did turn sixteen and seventeen and eighteen, all I had left were the dreams. When I looked in the mirror then, it was not my body I saw, but the more perfect one I had envisioned in my head.

Even now, each morning when I wake up in that half-conscious state between sleep and awareness, I am convinced that my feet and my body have been imbued with magic, that today will be the day they bend to my will and I can float above the world. But when I crawl out of bed, my bare heels hitting the icy-cold floor, I become aware of gravity again, the weight of my feet on the ground. I bend over and stretch, bring my nose to my knees, feeling the strain in the back of my calves.

Then I point my toes, look at the arch from side to side. Each day I am shocked all over again that I am the same as I was the day before. Each day the disappointment is fresh and new and raw.

People might say that it is unhealthy to court pain in this way. But I think to give up the dream itself would be much much worse, like pulling back Oz's curtain to see that the great wizard is only a meek, rather ordinary man.

So even though I told my parents, my friends, and even myself that my dance career is over—that the challenges of a writing life are something I am better suited for; even though I go to sleep thinking about the stories and voices in my head, somewhere in the middle of the night I slip back into the old dream.

So this afternoon in the studio dressing room, I wriggle into my black leotard with the neck cut down to form a sharp "V" right above my breasts. I pull my thick black tights up over my legs and fold the elastic waistband under five or six times until the thickness sits on the front of my hips, which helps to balance the appearance of my butt, which sticks out just a little too much in back.

I enter the dance studio. Dancers are everywhere in the room. Lovely, lovely long-limbed dancers sprawled all over the floor, stretching, talking, warming up their bodies. Here and there, a few of the dancers ice their feet after a tough modern dance class. The teachers say that ice reduces the swelling after an injury. The students use it in order to dull the pain so that they can keep on dancing.

While I tape up my third and fourth toes to prevent them from rubbing against the box of my *pointe* shoes, the dance department assistant hands each one of us a white slip of paper with a black number on it.

I am number eighteen. I pin the number on the waistband of my tights. I hate wearing a number. It makes me feel anonymous, even though when I came in to audition I filled out a white index card that in addition to my number also included my name, address, phone number, and days and times I'm available for rehearsal.

Though the faculty is auditioning dancers to perform in five different works, I only want to dance in Daria's piece. So do many of the other dancers in the room. I know that because one of them raises her hand and asks if she can only audition for a particular person.

We are told that everyone must complete the entire audition because it demonstrates our stamina, but that we don't have to wear *pointe* shoes if we only want to be in the modern pieces.

There is a sigh of relief from some of the students.

In the background, Gregory, our pianist, practices some music. I have recently become aware that Gregory is in love with Daria. During class, even as Gregory keeps one eye on the sheet music, he watches Daria's every move. Every day he tries to come up with a new piece of music, some inspired composition that will capture Daria's attention. Over the past few weeks, he has brought in various instruments to play—a Jew's harp, a zither, an African drum. Often he plays the piano while at the same time shaking a single maraca that he holds between his teeth. And when Daria does compliment his ability between combinations, he first grins, then blushes.

Since Gregory and I share the same lovesickness, perhaps I am more aware of how hard he tries to win her approval. None of the other dancers seem to find his behavior strange. They are just grateful to have an accompanist who seems truly in love with his job, someone capable of playing more than just the basic waltzes and quarter-time compositions that have always been the ballet world's mainstay.

Daria claps her hands and calls the audition to order. There will be two ballet pieces, one of which she will choreograph, and three modern works, including a restaging of Martha Graham's famous piece "The Shakers." Daria says that each choreographer will teach a few phrases from their works, which we will then present.

I feel my stomach muscles begin to tighten. I tell myself that none of this matters, that I'm here to become a better writer. I tell myself that I have the edge because Daria has known me for years, and she has only known the rest of the dancers in the group for a few weeks.

I close my eyes and breathe in deeply and try to send positive messages to Daria's brain.

Pick me, pick me, pick me...

Daria presents the first sixteen counts of a phrase. All forty-four of us learn it at once, standing in rows seven or eight abreast. Six male dancers are auditioning, so that actually brings my competition down to thirty-eight.

As Daria calls out our numbers to take our place on the floor, I watch each one of the girls carefully, measuring them up in my mind. I know that there are only nine whom I really have to worry about. And, of course, after four weeks of classes it is only those nine whose names I bothered to learn. The dancers less skilled than me pose no threat, aren't barriers to my happiness, and as such, are of little consequence.

Daria asks Gregory to halt his playing. She sticks a tape into the portable cassette recorder, so that we can hear the opening bars of the piece.

"It is very quick," she says. "You have to have really clean lines and still keep up with the tempo."

A few of the dancers giggle nervously.

"Numbers one through eight, take your place in the center, please."

I watch the faculty whispering to each other as the first group runs through the phrase over and over again. Occasionally, one of the teachers will point to a particular dancer and write something on one of those white index cards.

"Nine through eighteen, please."

I take my place on the floor. I try to will Daria to look at me. The tape begins. I draw in a deep breath.

Use the music, point the feet, round the arms, tilt the head, no, not that way, stupid, don't push out on the right hip, that's it, then contract the stomach, pirouette, walk, walk, walk...

"Next group, please."

As the audition progresses, the choreographers begin to switch us around, breaking down the steps, putting certain people together for reasons only they can see. Like shoppers at a fruit stand, they compare us for ripeness and beauty.

After twenty minutes, I am breathing quite hard. Pain rips through the first toe on my left foot, then I feel a sudden warmness. My toe, encased tightly in my *pointe* shoe, has been begun to bleed. My skin is clammy from sweat.

Suddenly, it is over. I feel great and terrible at the same time. You have to feel great after such a workout, the poisons working themselves out of your system. But at the same time, I remain anxious, knowing that it will be twenty-four hours until they post the cast lists.

I go home.

I shower, washing the sweat from my body. The hot water stings my sliced-open toe, but I welcome the pain.

I towel dry my hair. I throw on a robe.

I enter my room, grab the stack of student stories that I am supposed to comment on for my writing workshop. I read through each of the stories, crossing out lines, entire sentences that seem superfluous. I am merciless. It does not make me feel any better.

Somehow, the next day, I make it through my writing workshop, then my literature class. As I walk towards Meany Hall, I glance up at the third floor. My eyes move to the third window, to Daria's office. She is there, talking on the phone. I wave. She does not see me.

I tell myself that I will take ballet class before checking the list. That way, at least I won't ruin a perfectly good dance class.

But I know if I *don't* check, it will be ruined anyway.

I climb the three flights of stairs. I go to the bulletin board. The list is four pages long, each name typed in small black letters. I go immediately to Daria's page. I read the names over carefully. I read them over twice, thinking there must be some mistake.

My name does not appear. My heart falls into my belly like an elevator cut from its safety cord.

"Congratulations," I hear.

I look up from the bulletin board.

It is Daria. She is smiling. Of course, it must be a joke. She's picked me, but didn't want to put me on the list. She wanted to tell me in person.

"I'm very proud of you," Daria says. "Karol is looking forward to working with you."

"Karol?" I say. Karol Wies is the other ballet teacher in the department. He and Daria alternate teaching the advanced ballet class.

"Yes, he put you in his piece. Didn't you see your name?"

"I was looking somewhere else," I say.

My eyes meet hers.

"Come on," she says. "Time for class."

I know I should be thrilled. After all, I still get to perform. And Karol used to be the lead choreographer for the Spokane Ballet. But it hurts so. It hurts that Daria chose eight other dancers over me—seventeen- and eighteen-year-old girls whom she has only known a month or two—over me, whom she has known six years, and trained and talked to and advised.

All my life I've felt passed over. Growing up in a household of seven children, three of whom were adopted after my aunt and uncle died, competition for my parents' time, love, and energy, especially from my mother, who sometimes was so overwhelmed by it all she could scarcely get out of bed, was the standard mode of living. And then, in college, I was perpetually cast as the understudy or in a piece that even the choreographer seemed to have second doubts about.

I have met so many talented, extraordinary people in my life. Why hasn't the talent rubbed off?

In the movie *Amadeus,* the composer Salieri curses God for giving him the desire to create, and a fierce love of music, but not enough talent to bring that desire to life. "Mediocrity," he says about himself to the priest at the asylum at the film's end. "I christen thee in the name of Mediocrity."

Now I must go back into the dance studio, walk into Daria's class, and act as though I am fine, as though I do not see and wish so desperately to be these young thin girls with banana-shaped feet that look perfect in *pointe* shoes.

OCTOBER 24

I met a man named Brad Baldwin today in the computer lab while I was working on my Early American Lit paper. I overheard him making a reference to *The Scarlet Pimpernel,* one of my all-time favorite books and a great movie starring Jane Seymour and Anthony Andrews. He misquoted the character of Sir Percy to someone in the lab and I couldn't resist correcting him. (After all, what good is reading a novel twenty or thirty times if you can't use your knowledge?)

He laughed and told me that we were both in the same class. I looked at him amazed. There are only fifteen of us in Early American Lit and he is blond, tan, and incredibly good-looking, and likes nineteenth-century romances. In fact, he looks more like someone straight out of *Chariots of Fire* than a twenty-six-year-old man who grew up on a ranch in Montana. How does a rancher's kid learn to love William Thackeray? And how is it possible that after a month of classes, I never noticed him? Just look what I've been missing, wallowing in my self-absorbed daze, devastated by Daria.

After the lab closes, we go out for coffee (which I don't drink— but why let that stop me?). Then he offers to walk me back to my apartment. He has his bicycle which he rides to school every day. I carry his backpack full of books; he grabs hold of the handlebars and walks alongside me. As we walk the dark campus, the rhythm of the bike's spinning wheels merges with our conversation. I decide that I like the sound.

At my door, he asks for my phone number. "In case I have any questions about class assignments," he says.

I give it to him.

He asks me if I like all movies or just *The Scarlet Pimpernel.*
I laugh and say something clever about F. Scott Fitzgerald.
I think I say the quote about there being no second acts in American
lives. I'm sure he has no idea what I mean.

But Brad nods his head slowly. I hand him his backpack.
He swings it onto his broad shoulders.

I can scarcely breathe.

Then he is gone.

And I am back in my room, sitting against the wall on my
narrow slat of a bed, writing this all down, while on my stereo Janis
Ian sings of an approaching winter.

OCTOBER 27

It was just after 7:30. I had already taken my shower after a rather
rigorous ballet class; had, in fact, already devoured my plateful of
Kraft Macaroni and Cheese and a disappointingly dry apple.
Strange thing about the apples out here—Washington state is supposed to be apple capital of the world, but Macintoshes are nearly
impossible to find. And in the grocery store, all the Delicious are
stamped with a Canadian growers farm label. Someone told me that
all the best apples are shipped to the rest of the country,
so Washingtonians have to make do. Seems crazy to me—for a state
to be so money-hungry that it doesn't even keep some of its best
products for its own residents.

Anyway, I am struggling over the apple dilemma when my
phone rings. I answer it on the second ring.

It is he. Brad.

"There's a new John Sayles film playing up on Capitol Hill."
It starts in twenty-five minutes. Can you meet me there?"

"Now?" I say.

"Well, if you can't I understand."

"No," I say quickly, grateful my hair is nearly dry. "I can make
it. Where's Capitol Hill?"

He laughs, "I keep forgetting this is only your first year. You've lived here, what, a month now?"

"Five weeks," I say. "Is it far?"

"Catch a Number 7 or 9. There is a bus stop just up the street from you. Tell them you're going to the Broadway Theater. The bus driver will know when you should get off."

"Okay," I say. "But if I'm going to make it, I've got to hang up right now."

The phone goes dead.

I rush to my closet, looking for my soft royal-blue sweater, the one that feels like angora and discreetly reveals just a bit of bare shoulder. I slip it over my head and pull on a clean pair of jeans. I do my hair, hoping its slight dampness will keep it from blowing too much in the wind. I brush my teeth, stroke a thin line of coral lipstick over my mouth, and a single streak of blush on each cheek. I am ready in three minutes.

I grab a bit of change from my stack of quarters which I use for the laundromat in the basement of the housing complex. I have to ask one of my apartment mates how much the bus costs. So far, my entire universe has consisted simply of the places I can walk to—my job, the campus, and University Way.

I sling my purse over my arm, debate whether the warmth of a jacket is worth ruining the impact of the sweater. I decide if I carry the coat, swinging it over one shoulder, its wrinkly brown leather a sharp contrast to the soft blue wool, I will look both sensible and stylish.

At the bus stop, I wait six minutes, checking my watch every thirty seconds or so. The bus pulls up—I deposit my sixty cents. The driver hands me a yellow slip.

"What's this?"

"A transfer," he says.

"I need to transfer?" I panic suddenly. Brad hadn't said anything about transferring. "I'm going to Capitol Hill," I say. "The Broadway Theater."

"Okay, lady, so you don't need to transfer. No big deal."

The bus moves through the darkness—we passengers looking green as space aliens in the poor fluorescent lighting. We go over the University Bridge, which links the university to the rest of the city. Brad was right. It is a fairly short ride—in twenty minutes, I am outside the theater. He is standing in front of the marquee.

The movie is *Matewan* starring James Earl Jones. I love the rich resonance of Jones's voice and, while I remain fairly unmoved by the film plot (a coal miners' strike in West Virginia), I listen to him talk and try hard not to think about the man sitting beside me.

Afterwards, we stand awkwardly out in the street.

"What did you think?" he asks.

"B+," I say.

"Do you need to get back right away?" he asks.

I shake my head.

We walk down the street to a place called The Gravity Bar, which serves health food drinks—odd combinations like carrot-cabbage-beansprout juice. An eight-ounce glass costs $3.95 and I try to discreetly feel around in my purse to make sure I have enough cash.

I don't know whether or not to call what Brad and I are on a *date,* and even if we are I don't expect him to pay. I think I can manage it, so I order a strawberry-orange-lime smoothie.

We watch the bartender mix up a bluish concoction in a spaceage-looking blender. I am suddenly transported back to summer camp in New Hampshire when I was twelve.

To make the camp carnival a success, every bunk had to design and run an activity booth. The counselors had just taken us to see *Star Wars* at one of the theaters in Concord, so we decided to turn our booth into a travelers' bar, like the one in the movie where Luke Skywalker meets and hires Han Solo. We came up with weird-sounding names for drinks, like "Blue Moon Phantom," which we made by putting blue food coloring into milk, or "Mars Sunrise," a combination of cherry and lime Kool-Aid. We would sell each drink for ten cents.

But the night before the carnival, our bunk failed inspection because the counselors found a few black hairs in the bathroom sink. We were supposed to go put the finishing touches on our booth, but as punishment for the failed inspection, we had to clean the entire bunkhouse all over again.

We all grumbled a bit, and one of the girls blamed it on Maria, a Puerto Rican girl from Brooklyn who slept in the bottom bunk a few feet away from mine. I didn't like Maria much—she had thick calves and a rough tomboy attitude—and during the camp movie fest, she had the annoying habit of cracking her gum really loudly during the kissing scenes, which were my favorite parts of the film. But that night, some of the girls in my bunk crawled over to Maria's cot and cut off her hair while she slept.

The girls' whispers had awakened me, but I lay in my bed pretending to be asleep, my hands cold with fear. Each time I heard the scissors bite into Maria's thick silky hair, I flinched in empathy. After all, my hair was just as black as hers.

The next day, with Maria in tears, the counselors questioned each one of us in private to find the guilty party. But like every American kid, I knew that if a group of bullies wanted to exact revenge on somebody, a pair of sixteen-year-old counselors offered little protection. Sooner or later, at the lake where we had swim classes, in a remote corner of the softball field, or at the mess hall, the bullies would find me. And if the girls would cut off someone's hair just for having poor cleaning habits, what would they do to a tattletale? What would they do to me?

I kept thinking of the pictures I had seen in Hebrew school of the women in the concentration camps, faces etched with hunger and fear, their shorn heads covered with scabs from the cruel bite of a dull razor.

I also thought of my father, ever the New York liberal, who I knew would be very disappointed in me for doing nothing to stop the girls. "Now let's see, children," my father would say in his best lawyer-addressing-the-jury-voice. "Which is the greater wrong—those who commit crimes out of ignorance or prejudice, or those who know the crime is wrong, but stand by and do nothing to stop it?"

My father conducted such conversations with us often over our Sunday morning breakfast of bagels and lox, especially after he had just read an article in the *New York Times* about some injustice happening in South Africa or the Soviet Union. To my father, such issues were always quite clear—you helped those in need. But that day at camp, I realized that most issues are clear when you are not the person who has to choose what side to take.

So I did nothing. And even though there were two more weeks of the session left, camp ended for me that day. I continued to attend all the scheduled activities, responded when talked to, but I totally withdrew emotionally, thoroughly ashamed of myself for lacking the courage to do what I knew in my heart was right.

Instead, at night, I would read the discarded paperbacks of the counselors, racy stories of teen sex and mutilation by monsters, books I normally had no interest in. As long as I had words to concentrate on, a plot line to follow, I knew the girls would be powerless to hurt me. I floated through the campgrounds those last two weeks, watching everything that took place, but put my body away.

Now, suddenly here in the bar in Seattle, I remember how on the day of the carnival the milk in our Blue Moon Phantoms soured in the hot New Hampshire sun and the ice melted into our Mars Sunrise, watering down the taste. We didn't sell a single drink.

"Are you all right?" Brad asks me now.

"Excuse me?"

"You really zoned out. I asked you if you liked your drink."

I look at the gorgeous blond man next to me. So far, we have exchanged only a handful of words.

"Sorry," I say. I decide if he asks me what I was thinking about, I will confess—tell Brad about Maria and those odd strange moments that send you straight back into childhood, when you felt both powerful and helpless at the same time.

He does not ask.

"I had a really great time, Brad," I say. "But it is getting late. Will you walk me to the nearest bus stop?"

We get on the Number 7 and head back to the University District. We sit next to each other on the bus, not speaking. My stop comes way before his. I pull the yellow cord and stand up.

"Well, thanks for inviting me to the movie," I say.

"Yeah," he says. "It was cool."

I wait for him to ask me out again.

"See you around," he says.

"Yeah. See you."

I turn and walk down the aisle to the bus exit. I know it is too dark for Brad to see me, but just in case, I use my most graceful walk—the one I perfected in the hopes that someday I would get to dance the role of Giselle, the ghost woman who dies from want of love.

I realize that I am very good at being a ghost.

OCTOBER 30

Today I saw Brad standing outside Padelford Hall talking to a tall, dark-haired woman. I have no idea who she is but don't care. It is Brad I watch. Despite the damp overcast skies, the dominant weather pattern for Seattle, he is wearing a red rugby shirt and black bicycle shorts that beautifully display his well-muscled calves.

Looking at him takes my breath away. In New York and in Boston, I've taken classes with some of the top male dancers in the country, yet none of them were as beautiful as Brad.

I can see that the woman Brad talks to also finds him beautiful, because she looks only at him, as though amazed that such a man really exists. She does not see me approach.

But Brad does. I see it register in his eyes.

I slow down my pace as I approach the building, smile, and give him a wave. I take a step towards them.

Yet suddenly as I near them, Brad is on his bike and in a blur passes me by. I know he saw me.

I do not understand. I do not understand. I do not understand.

OCTOBER 31

I call Rachel on the phone. We talk about her job as associate producer for the Mount Holyoke Summer Theater. We talk about the latest man in her life. He is a photographer, does the publicity photos for the theater, and has just divorced.

"He's having a bad time of it," Rachel says.

Rachel provides him sympathy but tells me that they are only friends. I know that means that she likes him, that she wants it to be something more. She may not know it yet, but I can tell by her voice and the way she talks about him.

This is how Rachel and I communicate.

I tell her about Brad.

She asks me how I feel.

"I think I am falling in love with him," I say and mean it.

"How does he feel about you?" she says.

"I have no idea."

"That's the challenge, isn't it?" she says.

"Yes."

And we laugh. We laugh about men and us and how crazy it all is, and I feel better.

NOVEMBER 1

Woke from an exhausting night of dreaming: images of projected stories, completed novels, images of the movies I saw last night at the local rerun house (*Mosquito Coast* and *The Year of Living*

Dangerously), images of Brad and images of old lovers, all merging together, coming at me like a living Dali painting.

I observed it all just like a film, feeling the emotions I was supposed to feel, but playing no role in the action that appeared before me.

This was a dream about longing, about possibility, equipped with dialogue and plot. It was a disturbing dream, but not one from which I wanted to wake. I left reluctantly, perhaps because the *script* was in place. In the dream, at least, everything seemed settled, everything belonged.

NOVEMBER 3

I have gone to the movies three times with Brad now. It is always the same. He calls me at the last minute, names a theater and a time, and then we meet.

In this way, I feel that I am starting to get to know the city better, since these theaters—big cavernous spaces with names like the Neptune or the Egyptian that have been declared historical landmarks—are vested in the early culture of Seattle.

I haven't asked Brad about that time in front of Padelford Hall when he pretended he didn't see me, because the opportunity never seems right.

He never seems to tell me anything, actually. Nothing personal, that is. I know as much about him now as I did a month ago.

But I thought tonight all that might change. For the first time, he invited me (on a weekend no less) to come over to his place to watch *Saturday Night Live*. I know the TV show doesn't end until one in the morning, so I tell Brad that it is much too late for me to take the bus back alone, but he promises if I come over that he will drive me back in his friend's car, which he has borrowed for a few days.

This is the first time Brad has gone out of his way to have me see him, so I take it as a sign of good things to come. I've also decided that if tonight he does not kiss me, I will know that he only wants to be friends.

I could live with that, once I know.

But I can't be imagining the electricity between us. You can't fake attraction, or hide from it—and despite my relatively few lovers, I know that it is rare that only one half of the couple feels it. One person may love another without reciprocity, but by its very definition sexual attraction always involves two.

So I dress carefully, and slip the white plastic case containing my diaphragm into my purse. After all, it's best to be prepared.

I'm not being blasé, but while some people claim that using a diaphragm spoils spontaneity, not having any birth control around spoils a mood even more. Especially when part of me is not sure why I am putting myself through all this.

Anyway I take the bus to Brad's place, which is about six miles from campus.

He lives alone except for a giant collie named Percy (after Sir Percy Blakeney of *The Scarlet Pimpernel*, of course). I am afraid of dogs, especially big furry ones that think they are people. When dogs stand on their legs, they are usually taller than I am. I worry that a dog will jump on me and I will suffocate in their fur.

That's what it feels like when I'm in a room with a dog, that I'm suffocating, that I cannot breathe. But Brad loves his dog, talks about him all the time, so I have to pretend that I like Percy too. And after a few initial barks at the door when Brad lets me in, Percy does back off and lies down in a corner near the TV in the living room. Throughout the night, however, we eye each other warily.

While Brad gets me a ginger ale, I check out the books on his bookshelves. There is surprisingly little fiction, just a few paperback novels, but most of the books are on criticism. I comment on this.

"I've gotten really tired of reading fiction," Brad says. "It bores me now. I'm much more interested in literary criticism."

"Like who?" I say.

"The French mostly. Derrida, of course. Barthes. Lacan. But mostly Michel Foucault. I'm really into Foucault."

I wince.

When I was nineteen, I took a summer course at the city college near my parents' house. Because Mount Holyoke's standards were much higher than the local school's, I was allowed to enroll in a graduate seminar, which happened to be my first true introduction to literary criticism.

So I read a bit of Claude Levi-Strauss and of Derrida and Foucault, as well as a half-dozen other critics. I learned the terminology: structuralism, post-structuralism, deconstruction, reconstruction, but never quite understood what the attraction was. To me, breaking down paragraphs into words and syllables and then putting them all back together again feels too much like arithmetic—an attempt to make science out of literature.

I think that's why literary criticism tends to come out of the universities and graduate schools rather than the liberal arts colleges—the university English departments feel the need to compete with their colleagues at the schools of medicine, law, and engineering for research dollars.

While I admit that taking a Marxist, Freudian, Darwinian, or feminist viewpoint can often help illuminate a text historically or politically, I never thought that deconstructing language necessarily helped me understand the author's meaning any better.

It's almost as though the English professors are ashamed that there are no systematic formulas—that literature is contradictory, because the writers who wrote the books are human and themselves contradictions.

But that's what I love about books—about novels. That's what comforts me late at night when I cannot sleep and my thoughts race. It comforts me to know that other writers struggle with their humanity.

Meanwhile, I realize that Brad is waiting for some response. I want to say that when I write I choose particular words in a particular order because they sound right or reveal something telling about a character. I don't stop to think about what the words might mean if broken down by vowel sounds (though I think it's different for poetry), and what that says about me politically or socially.

I think a lot of writing happens by accident. That a writer struggles to get a particular passage right, to help illuminate character or theme, and suddenly she realizes that the passage also symbolizes the evils of greed or capitalism or something. The passage may not be what she originally intended, but that's what's great about creativity—sometimes the creative self is smarter than the conscious self, sometimes the creative self knows what to do even when you don't.

Those are the moments that make me grateful, those are the moments when I feel that if there is a God, I've gotten as close to union with him or her or it as I'm going to get.

I want to say all this to Brad, but I don't, because I am afraid that if I do he will laugh, or still worse, say what others have often said to me—that I have no right to expect more than what most people have, that to expect more will only bring disappointment.

"Kiss me," I say to Brad now.

And he does—kisses my lips and my neck and ear—and I kiss him back.

There are minor explosions rather than fireworks, but our kisses are fleshy and human and real and temporarily obliterate all my fears.

Of course, we end up in bed, but he does not come inside of me—I've forgotten to tell him that I have slipped in my diaphragm in the bathroom, and by the time I do, he has already come on the sheets.

"Well, well," he says.

"Well," I say.

"You're fun to existentially pet with," he says.

"Am I?" I say.

"Sure," he says, and reaches for his pants.

Existential petting?

I am very, very grateful I did not tell Brad about my sometime union with God.

NOVEMBER 5

He is involved with someone else.

Last night at his place, while he was kissing me, the phone suddenly rang. The way he answered it, the way he talked to the voice on the phone, suddenly explained everything.

I had wondered before if he hadn't come inside me because he somehow thought that would prevent pregnancy or disease—but now I think that he did not come inside me because in that way he still remains faithful to her.

I asked him if I was right.

He didn't even look sheepish, just said that they are "on again-off again" like a roller-coaster ride. He also said it was hard to end something when there is a past, but that he found me attractive, intelligent, and very free, so thought I would understand.

But I don't understand. I don't understand why I tend to always be the "second" woman. With Pete and Adam, it was their wives, with Hugo it was his ex-girlfriend, his work, and my own pride.

Perhaps it is me, perhaps I *allow* myself to be second, to give all of myself to the man and get only parts of them in return?

Rachel tells me that I should have more self-respect, hold out for a man who is truly free to love me. But until recently, I never really wanted someone of my own; the man's marriage always kept the relationship both safe and exciting.

But this time, I said no. I told Brad that I was not as free as he thought I was, but I liked him a lot, and if he resolved his conflict with his girlfriend Juleen he should call me. For once I said no.

Then I left, and now I feel utterly, utterly alone.

I watch him in class. I note when he arrives and whom he sits next to. Always a woman. Never next to me.

While the professor talks about Charles Brockden Brown and the gothic novel *Wieland* (a very odd book, by the way), I stare at Brad. If he suddenly happens to glance up and meet my eye, I pretend that I am taking notes.

And in a way I am: I note if his face looks worn and tired like mine. I wonder if late at night he lies in bed with his girlfriend and thinks of me, or sees my face on the monitor of his computer.

I note all this and feel a fool.

Angry, angry—so angry at myself for letting a man disrupt my goals, disrupt my work.

Perhaps I am not really in love with Brad, only in love with the idea of loving him. Yet it takes so little for me to love a man— usually just the fact that he doesn't love me back is enough.

When I think of him, my heart speeds up and there is a tightening in my stomach. Not mere excitement at seeing him, but more, an acute ache, the knowledge that I mean little to him.

I know it was my choice. I told him I could not see him as long as he was involved with Juleen.

Still, I wait for him to call. I wait each night in anticipation and then grow furious with myself for waiting.

I watch him in class, flirting with some of the older women, and I want to call out, "What do you want from me? See me, really see me. There is far, far more to me than what you want to see. I am a woman through and through: I want to be soft, I want to be kind, I want you to like me; I want you to like my mind, my soul—my body you have already had. I feel stifled by you simply because you won't allow me to be who I am and because I don't have the strength to tell you to leave me alone."

I've gotten nowhere with him.

Oh, what's wrong with me that he can't love me?

Be careful what you ask for … so the old axiom goes.

I was here all alone watching TV, feeling overstuffed after eating an entire portion of take-out chicken teriyaki, when the doorbell rang.

Yes, it was him. Brad. I looked a mess—khakis, an old sweater, my hair not brushed. And it was him.

He claimed he lost my phone number, or he would have been in touch sooner.

He swept in here like a storm, we played Janis Ian records, we made love, real love, for the first time. And then he left. All of this happened in a span of an hour and a half.

Before he left, he said, "I am supposedly the happiest I've ever been … with her."

Supposedly?

"If you're so happy," I said, "what are you doing here?"

"I wanted your phone number."

Not "I wanted to see you," not even "I wanted you." I wanted your phone number.

And when he left at the gray door, he did not kiss me goodbye. He did not say, "I'll see you" or "I'll call you."

Yet, for whatever reason, be it lust, curiosity, or the power game, he is attracted to me; there was some reason that he came to me tonight and not to the girlfriend—not to Juleen.

I know I should be furious, but it was just so totally unexpected, I was so sure that I had seen the last of him that I am more stunned than anything else. (I never react correctly to the unexpected, perhaps a throwback to my childhood, when the unexpected always meant disaster—my mother's bitter, angry outbursts, my aunt's death from liver cancer, my uncle suffering a heart attack totally without warning—and my response was always either to blame myself or block the pain out.)

Do these things happen to other women? They must. Yet Camden Dearborn and the other writers in workshop accuse me of writing melodrama.

But look at my life, at least at my love life—it's out of an over-acted movie, real only because it is happening to me.

NOVEMBER 19 (Midnight)

I must record the events that happened in writing workshop today. Lisa Barstow, one of the students, wrote a story about an American woman who goes to help the poverty-stricken in Haiti and about her inability to help or fit in there.

Anyway, it was a wonderful idea for a story (I love what Joan Didion does with ideas like this), but unfortunately it wasn't well written. I think most of the class felt that way, too, because the comments got more and more negative. Someone said that the black characters in the story were stereotyped. And then someone said something about racist writing.

All of us are very vulnerable as we lay our lives, albeit fictionalized, before a not always gentle audience.

Lisa exploded, took the comments extremely seriously, extremely personally. She is a journalist at the *Seattle Times,* always dressed in dark suits, a bit too plastic-looking. She was on the brink of tears, but pride kept her together long enough to pick herself up and walk out of class in the middle of it all. I do not know if I admire her for this or not. I do know the feeling that drove her to do it.

Afterwards, of course, everyone acted a bit sorry. Dearborn, who did nothing to contain the conversation earlier, made a big speech about sensitivity and thinking more about each other's feelings. He asked us all to personally call Lisa and invite her back to class.

I was outraged but kept my mouth shut. This entire workshop is about pulling people's work apart. I do not doubt that all of us have felt as put upon and disliked as Lisa did today. Yet Dearborn and the class cry crocodile tears. If Lisa had stayed to take it, like the rest of us have done, swallowing our pain, no one would have made such statements about the need to be more sensitive.

There have been dance classes—far too numerable to count, in fact—that have left me in tears. And I have felt scathing anger in writing seminars at the other class members, the teachers, myself. It takes a very deep conviction in your work, and a strong but flexible constitution, to withstand the blows of the critics' comments.

Still, I am amazed that somehow I am stronger than Lisa, stronger than this hotshot journalist who has won a few awards at the paper. I could take it and she could not.

Do I despise her for this? Maybe. Will I call her and beg her to come back? No. If she really wants to be a fiction writer, she will have to find the strength within herself. Otherwise the same thing will just happen again.

If this makes me uncompassionate, then I am uncompassionate. But I cannot be party to Dearborn's hypocrisy. (Does he really think that after asking her to come back, anyone will ever be objective or truthful about her work again?) Lisa must want to succeed as a writer on her own.

A nasty business this, being writers and critics and students and readers all rolled into one.

NOVEMBER 22

Read Hannah Foster's *The Coquette* for my Eighteenth-Century American Lit class. Though the roles of women and the rules of love and sex are completely different today, I could not help feeling that whether a woman is rejected by a whole society (as in the book) or merely by a single man, the feeling of self-recrimination remains. We tend to blame ourselves. Men tend to blame others.

Yes, on the surface men and women appear equal today; a woman no longer is thought to be a "bad" person if she chooses to have sex with a man before marriage. But simply because we attach so much emotional import to the relationship, to making love, we are still in chains, unequal.

Why oh why can I not stop talking about men? I have spent so much of my time with women; I have admired and loved many of them, but it is from men that I have learned. When I am with other women I feel very much a person. But it is only when I am with a man that I become completely aware of myself as a woman, as female. I do not know if this is good or bad, feminist or rather old-fashioned; I only know what I feel.

There are some men who will only make love to women they care about, and there are women who attach no emotional importance to sex. But I've never met either of these types.

Perhaps my friend Tracey, whom I'm going to visit over the Thanksgiving holiday, comes close to fitting in the latter category, except that I know underneath her blasé attitude, underneath the two abortions she's already had, there is a fierce, deep-seated anger. She uses the anger to her advantage; nonetheless, it is there and real and directed towards herself.

NOVEMBER 23

I had an idea today for mixing my writing with my dancing—a sort of multimedia project. Perhaps it was that painting Gloria did of me that made me think of it, or simply being in dance class and hearing about the student dance concert and desperately missing performing.

I am no choreographer, but I could write a good script, an interesting, slightly humorous, slightly sad script, overlay it with original music (I would need to get someone to write a score), and then put dancers on stage, not telling the script or acting it out, but dancing the images that the words evoke. Maybe this is the only way to have "Beauty" (the character I thought of a few weeks ago) speak.

Nothing at all technique-oriented, but the mood, the movement the words brought to the surface.

It is a challenging task, but one that intrigues me. If I could write it over Christmas, find a composer, I could rehearse it for the spring concert. I will never again have the resources that the university offers: dance studios, stage, dancers, and musicians all available for free.

My mind more and more turns towards performance-oriented work. A straightforward play, this dance idea. It is not that conventional writing (i.e., short stories, novels) bores me, but stories are a personal private event, written alone and then read alone. Physical connection is what excites me, as does immediate response. I do not know if I have the patience to be a novelist. I don't lack the patience to write novels, but perhaps lack the patience necessary to wait a very long time for a reaction to my work.

NOVEMBER 24

My telephone has not rung in days. And every afternoon, the mailbox remains empty. How easily we can become isolated. And yet, at the same time, I marvel that three thousand miles can be bridged so quickly. Next week, for Thanksgiving, I fly to California to see my friend Tracey. It is a mere two-hour flight. And then tonight on TV, watching the news, they flashed, as they always do, the sports scores. Boston, Chicago, etc. Fifty states, hundreds of cities. What makes a country, especially a country so large, a country? What keeps it from falling apart into a thousand pieces?

The news is bad, yes, always bad, a stupid, blinded president, a conservative government, welfare, poverty, murder, rape, drugs, not to mention a rapidly deteriorating environment. But somehow life at the university goes on, goes on in Seattle, in Boston and New York.

I read in the *New York Times* that ten people a day are dying of AIDS in New York City. It is hard to imagine that and yet not so hard. I can so easily picture one death, an individual death, a man or a woman dying alone in an antiseptic hospital or still worse, at home, where reminders of how they used to be surround them. I know I can imagine my death, even once tried to bring it about. Why is it then so horrifying to imagine only nine more?

In a city so large, in a country so vast, who will notice? What is one more person more or less? These nameless people are all part of a crazy statistic of death.

For every day I live here in Seattle—as I worry about dance classes, writing, and growing ugly, growing sad—ten people die in New York. And how many others in Africa? In China and India? One person dies, another lives, and somewhere else another is just being born. How is it decided who lives or dies? Or is victim or survivor?

Is it really as random as it seems?

NOVEMBER 26 (Santa Cruz, California)

Looking out onto the sea and feeling strangely troubled. Tonight Tracey introduced me to her Argentine boyfriend, a man who, she says, is illegally working here on a tourist visa. He's a dishwasher at a Mexican restaurant, doing research, he says, about the American poor. Tracey admires him because he is a revolutionary—interested in someday overthrowing his government and building a socialist, freer state.

I have never met a revolutionary before, although in the early fifties, after my father graduated from Harvard Law School, he was denied a commission in the army because he supposedly had joined a "communist" drinking club in college.

"I think I went to two or three meetings," my father used to joke. "I heard that Communist girls were more likely to sleep with guys than the other girls on campus."

"Oh, Alan," my mother would say. But then she would laugh and take my father's hand.

After all, being a supposed Red brought my parents together. Because the army felt sending my father to Korea posed a security risk, he completed his military service in New Jersey, where he just happened to meet my mother on a blind date. So I've always had a soft spot for revolutionaries, especially when my father told me some not so very funny stories about what life was really like for many Americans under McCarthyism.

Yet, when I met Tracey's boyfriend, I felt afraid. Some people may admire a man who has defied his wealthy Argentine parents to come to the U.S. and wash dishes and risk being caught by the police. Perhaps even at one time I would have written about such a man and seen him as a hero, ready to give his life for his people.

But when Tracey was out of the room, he asked me questions about my writing and graduate school. I said that I was looking for the correlation between pure emotion and pure language, hoping to find a way to keep one from corrupting the other.

He laughed, dismissed my work as "bourgeois."

I laughed, too, though somewhat hollowly, and asked if such words weren't a bit out of style in late-twentieth-century America.

He views the world and himself as, as he says, "animalistic." People's attempt at civility is a lie, he says, only a mask people wear so that they can get what they really want.

"What do people really want?" I ask.

"Wine. Sex. Food. A place to sleep."

"No love?" I ask.

"Love is a bourgeois concept," he says. "To justify the upper classes' desire to merge property through marriage."

Oh please... Has this guy watched *Ninotchka* like a hundred times? Yet Tracey laughs when he speaks, her eyes glowing, talking about how with him she can live only for the moment.

He and Tracey too want to make it simple, make life as one dimensional as possible, describing the world in monosyllables: shit, fuck, dick, food, booze, drugs, real, fake.

If you choose to see life as simple as that, I suppose then that love really doesn't have any relationship with "fucking," and satiated with drugs or alcohol, as they have both been all weekend, one can say they are living for the moment.

Yet how dare anyone tell me the vision that I see is less real simply because I seek Life through the intangible?

DECEMBER 1 (Seattle)

My concentration has been totally destroyed. Words and images of Santa Cruz keep flooding through me, interrupting whatever I attempt. The magnificent copper-colored rock formations, granite covered with green moss and purple flowers, the stone carved out by the Pacific, the power, the immutability of nature.

The power a man has over a woman simply because he is physically stronger. The anger of helplessness.

I see his dark face, his penis growing hard in his blue jeans, his lips shiny with Vaseline, his face coming towards me.

I write that I see this all—but I know I did not. He blindfolded me, pinioned my hands behind my back so that I could not move.

But his words—I did hear his words, each one as it cut through me, stabbed my heart, just as his stiff penis tried to probe my insides. "Feel me. This is real. All else is bullshit. Your work is nothing."

The force in those words, his conviction that he is right. How does one fight that? How does one stop the face from coming at you again and again, those hands painfully running over your body, demanding of you, asking that you submit your will to his?

Danger, madness, anger—will the rage never leave me?

It is not that my heart has been broken. It has been cut out and replaced by hatred.

"Nothing," he said to me. "Say you are nothing."

And I am. For I am no longer my own person. I only exist now in terms of my anger and hatred towards him, the isolation I feel, how this man's fierce will, his own sick need to conquer, to overwhelm, has taken control of my life.

DECEMBER 2

I should have gone to the police. But they would ask me to describe him and all I would be able to say is that he told me I was nothing. All I would be able to say is that I screamed very, very loudly, and finally, before he could complete what he started, Tracey came and stopped it.

All I would be able to say is that after Tracey came and stopped it, she told me that I had misunderstood him. She told me that he thought I was sad because I didn't have a lover.

"Where did he get that idea?" I asked.

"Well, you know how you are. So serious. I mean, you never let yourself have any fun. I just thought he was going to flirt a little. Make you forget things."

"Flirt? For God's sake, Tracey, he tried to ra..."

"Don't," she said. "Don't say it. Don't even think it."

I should have gone to the police, but instead I took an early flight back to Seattle. Why go to the police? If Tracey can betray me, why should I trust strangers not to?

DECEMBER 3

Listening to the rain drop off the gray cement of the building. It is almost a crackling sound, a pop. Like fire. Fire and water. But I *know* it is rain. Yet if I was to suspend my belief?

Are you listening to me? This is all you have left me now, these words and this book to fill it up with. Shall I tell you about the flashbacks, about how I see your dark face looming before me over and over again?

You are walking now through the streets of Santa Cruz, your chapped lips covered with a smear of Vaseline, you walk the streets of the city, filled with your own self-importance, strolling the streets, unafraid.

You have power. You have control. You are a man. And you have your penis to prove it.

DECEMBER 6

After avoiding me for three weeks, even going so far as to miss lit class not to run into me, Brad called and asked me to a movie. As though none of the things that have happened ever occurred. As though there was no Juleen, no avowals from me not to see him again, no long silences.

And then, out it spilled. For the first time, I heard true emotion in Brad's voice—no longer prefacing his statements with quotes from Foucault or Lacan.

Brad simply said, "My aunt just died. I spent every summer on her ranch. She's the one who really raised me, not my parents. Now she is dead."

I am stunned. Over the phone, I hear his pain and wish I could help.

"Where's Juleen?" I ask, hating myself.

"Look," Brad says. "What about tonight? I've got to go to Montana tomorrow for the funeral."

"I'm sorry," I say, knowing this is inadequate.

"This is the first person I've ever known to die," Brad says.

I envy him suddenly, that his pure blond soul has managed to stay untainted, free of the images of hospital sick rooms, the overwhelming smell of piney antiseptic in your nose, watching your once beautiful aunt wither up from cancer. You watch from the corner of the hallway because your parents won't let you in the room to see her, though you are never sure whether it is because they don't want you to witness her pain or because they fear your noisy child self will disturb her. Instead, you and siblings watch from afar, hear the moans rising up from the bed, the hushed whispers of the grown-ups debating what steps to take in a treatment they know is failing. You are terrified, yet every week when your parents ask you if you really want to come, you cannot say no, you cannot stay away, endlessly fascinated by the incredible shrinking woman who grows smaller and smaller in the bed. Your imagination fills in what your eye cannot see and perhaps you think this is what death is—a shrinking away until you simply disappear into the sterile white sheets—until six months later, when your uncle drops dead of a heart attack in the middle of a medical conference, you learn that death can also be instantaneous.

For a few terrifying years, you get ill every time your parents leave the house, go out to dinner or see a movie, because now you know that it's possible they may not come back. Sometimes you get so ill that your stomach blows up with gas and they have to come home from the dinner party or the game of bridge they are playing at your father's partner's house, so that they can take care of you. Your father rubs your tummy, and even though your mother dutifully makes you dry toast and pours you a glass of flat ginger ale, you can also see she is angry at you for making her come home from one of her very infrequent nights out, especially now with three more children living in the house since your aunt's and uncle's deaths.

Then a few years later, you take the phone call on April Fool's Day from a hospital nurse who tells you to run quickly and fetch your parents because your favorite grandfather is dead, the one who used to pick you up from ballet class or drive you to Hebrew school because your mother didn't have time. The panic you feel because there is no one home to tell; you are twelve years old and you have to keep the secret all to yourself. And when your parents finally come home an hour later, your mother doesn't believe you. She accuses you of lying, of pulling an April fool.

Then there are other images that hurt a bit less. The wheeze of the organ at the funeral parlor as people whom you never met before walk up to you and shake your hand and tell you how sorry they are for your loss. The frightening sounds of adults falling apart, crying hysterically, when they are the ones who are supposed to be strong. The black limousines waiting to take you and your family to the graveyard, the gaping hole in the dirt as the walnut casket is lowered in.

Brad knows none of this, and while I envy him, I also feel somewhat smug about my knowledge of death, the way children often feel when they know the punchline to a bad joke.

Only now I am not a child anymore, so I do the only thing that I can think of to do. "We should go see a movie," I say. "We should go see the silliest movie we can think of and sit through it twice."

So we go see *The Princess Bride* up at the Varsity. It's a lovely movie, actually. Both making fun of romance and treasuring it at the same time.

We sit in the dark together. He does not touch me; I do not touch him, but at least he isn't alone.

He needed me tonight. It was me that he called. And it was the one thing that I knew I could do for him. I couldn't talk to him about grief—neither his nor my own (how can one talk about something that clings to you like a second skin?), but we could keep each other from being alone.

December 19 (New York)

I have been "home," back at my parents' house in Long Island, for twenty-four hours. I don't know why my mother always plans these large family reunion-type dinners, for they always make her anxious and short-tempered, constantly complaining that no one is doing a thing to help her. She always says this when my sisters and I are already working in the kitchen, getting the good china down from where it is stowed away, or polishing the silver.

I guess what she means is that my *father* isn't helping, that my father is in the living room reading the *New York Times* and talking with my grandmother. The thing is that my father would be happy to help her, but two hours before, she told him that it was his birthday so he should relax. More likely, she told him to make sure that he kept her mother out of my own mother's hair.

So the dinner went as these dinners always go—everyone talking way too fast, too much food that we will be eating as leftovers for days, and my mother finally sitting down at the table and announcing that she is so tired she can't move. Then somewhere between the second round of coffee and raspberry jelly roll and the seemingly endless stacking of dirty dishes into the sink and dishwasher, my older sister drifts towards the old Baldwin upright and begins to pick out Rodgers and Hammerstein show tunes.

"Raindrops on roses and whiskers on kittens…"

By the second chorus, eight or nine people are gathered around the piano. I love these old songs. As we grew up, my parents filled us up with MGM musicals and old Cary Grant movies the way some parents indulged their children with chocolate bars. Nonetheless, I come over to the piano slowly now, reluctantly, also remembering that in the past this brief moment of joy was often followed by one of my mother's bitter outbursts, a diatribe against my father or sometimes one of us kids for not appreciating all she did. (It wasn't until recently that I've begun to speculate that the outbursts after these mini-concerts resulted from her frustration at having to give up music, something she desperately loved, in part because of marriage to my father, but mostly because at seventeen she suffered from German measles and sustained a gradual but ever-increasing hearing loss.)

I come reluctantly to the piano for another reason as well. While I love these old songs, unlike many of my siblings and adopted siblings, I have not inherited my mother's ability to carry a tune. Even now, all grown-up when it should no longer matter, it hurts me still to see my sisters wince when I open my mouth to join in. Perhaps that is why I keep silent, why I write these words on a white blank page, working to perfect them, instead of letting them spill out to the world in a discordant rush of noise. I fear the world's collective wince.

Perhaps my little sister Linda does too, because later that night, as we all prepare for bed, I hear her in the bathroom talking to herself. The shower is running; she doesn't realize that it amplifies the sound. "Stupid," she says aloud. "That was very stupid of you." Then she slaps herself. Hard. Berating herself for some sin or mistake she feels she must have committed.

I want to rush in and tell her to stop. To not treat herself this way. I feel maternal towards her suddenly. My kid sister with the near-perfect SAT scores, with the scholarship to the University of Chicago. My sister who refuses to eat take-out because the Styrofoam packaging harms the environment.

I want to rush in and tell her to stop, but I do nothing for fear of embarrassing her. I also know that because I have witnessed, even though unintentionally, her private moment of self-doubt, that sooner or later, perhaps next week over the phone when she has gone back to Chicago and I've gone back to Seattle, I will call her and tell her about Santa Cruz. Matching secret for secret? A way to keep the score even, that there should be a sense of fair play even about witnessing someone during their weakest moments?

In the meantime, I make plans to be gone for the next few days. Away from my family, this fiercely loving, fiercely demanding family. After all, I am the dancer, the one who moves. The one who moved away.

Tomorrow I will spend the whole day with friends—Tuesday with Nathan in the city and then off to Rachel's in Boston.

DECEMBER 22

Saw Streisand's *Nuts* tonight. It's funny how often a film or a book gives me insight into my current life just when I need it most.

In the film, the defendant Claudia draws pictures, pictures of people without any mouths. If they don't have mouths, they can't tell the secrets they know. And now, less than four weeks after Santa Cruz, I have yet one more secret. One more thing that I cannot tell anyone, not even Rachel and certainly not my sister: I went to visit Nathan Katz (whom I met at Mount Holyoke when he served as a writer-in-residence) at his Manhattan apartment and I tumbled into a hornet's nest of lies and self-deception.

Nathan's second child is due to be born any day now, yet when I went to visit him at his apartment, his wife and daughter were nowhere to be seen. It was only Nathan, Nathan and his vast aching need to tell me something—to confess.

He looked different than I remembered. Back at Mount Holyoke, we would meet every Wednesday for lunch and he would go over my writing with me, sometimes line by line, telling me what did and did not work. Most of the time he was right, and after lunch I always went back to my dorm and rewrote the pages that same day.

I loved our lunches together my senior year. I loved them because they made me feel grown-up. Nathan took my work seriously. He viewed me as a writer, told me about writers in New York, editors he knew. He even introduced me to some of his friends, all rather well-known intellectuals, who often included me in their rather noisy discussions, questioning me about my views on contemporary fiction.

But now, three years later, here in his New York apartment, it was different. He was restless, endlessly paced the small living room—a room packed with books, thick heavy wooden bookcases, five of them stacked side by side, lining the walls all the way into the foyer. Old heavy books with gold-embossed printing on their red, blue, and green cardboard covers.

He paced, offered me some tea, which I wound up making myself in his tiny kitchen (because halfway through he forgot what he was doing).

"Nathan," I said. "Is something wrong?"

"I have to tell you something," he said.

I thought he was going to tell me that the story I sent him stinks, that Seattle had turned me into an awful writer.

He took my hand and sat me down next to him on the sofa. Then I noticed the small packet of white powder sitting next to a half-melted scotch and water. He did a few lines of coke in front of me, snorted it right up his nose.

I had never seen anyone take coke before, but I knew it wasn't his first time. He used to tell me about some of the parties he and his friends had. I used to listen enviously as he talked about some post-book-signing party at Elaine's, imagining myself walking into the famed restaurant with the self-assurance of someone who belonged, the quintessential successful New York writer.

He must've thought it was the parties I envied rather than the self-assurance, that I thought it cool his taking drugs in front of me, because I had never objected to his talking about it.

But it was not cool. I was uncomfortable and afraid. I suddenly felt every inch of my nice Jewish suburban upbringing. "Priss," I told myself. "Weenie. Open yourself up. A writer needs experience. Handle this. It's no big deal."

So I gave Nathan a smile and sat back deeper in the couch.

"You're not afraid to see the world for what it is, Sandi, are you? It's what I like most about you. I see it in your work—you don't duck from the truth."

I'm instantly flattered, stretching into the praise until I feel it comfortably wrapped around me like a pair of leggings.

"What is it that you want to tell me, Nathan?"

"Actually, I'd rather just show you. It's a project I'm working on. I want your honest opinion."

"Sure," I said.

Then he put a film in his VCR, which turned out to be a montage of sex scenes. The first one made me especially uncomfortable since the scenario was of a schoolteacher and her wayward student whom she kept after school for being bad. It felt too much like Nathan and me discussing my writing after class—at least it did until the schoolteacher opened her legs so that the student could see her pantyless crotch. Nathan watched me carefully as the teacher and student begin screwing on the desk. Then he showed me a series of pictures from *Hustler* and *Playboy*. He said that he wanted to see my reaction—that this was his project, studying what aroused people sexually. He kept asking me if I found the images offensive.

I looked at him. He was listening to me carefully, his restlessness gone—a thick heavy silent expectation. This wasn't a project,

I realized. This was something deeply, deeply personal. He *craved* these women.

"I've been thinking about a character lately," I said. "She doesn't have a name. I call her Beauty. She is a silent character, her head filled up with the voices of other people's expectations. I've been thinking about her a lot. I know it has to do with dancing— the perfect body moving through space and time, moving through music, but no words. Anyway, that's what these women remind me of—bodies without words, bodies without thoughts. I guess I am afraid I'm like them."

He went to put his arm around me.

"Don't," I said.

"I won't hurt you," he said.

"Nathan, I should go now."

"Don't go. It's just that I can't believe you just told me all that. You just said all that about yourself, just blurted it out."

"But you asked me. You told me to tell you the truth."

"I can't talk about my feelings when I'm dressed," he said suddenly. "I want to tell you about what turns me on. I need to tell you."

My heart pounded and I thought of Santa Cruz and then of those naked women in the video, opening themselves up to penetration, their holes being filled up with someone else's desire.

I looked around the room quickly, scanning its overcrowded bookshelves for a telephone, to call someone who might rescue me. But who would I call, and what would I say?

That I hated Nathan now. That I hated being in the apartment with him, hated what he had shown me, hated acting like I was mature and cool and with-it. Most of all that I hated myself. I still do as I write this. Twice in less than three months I have allowed myself to be caught up in a dangerous, impossible situation. In Santa Cruz, I hated that man the minute I laid eyes on him but stayed out of politeness to Tracey. At Nathan's I stayed because he writes for two of the biggest drama shows on television, has published three novels and regularly writes for *Rolling Stone* magazine. I stayed because Nathan had access to New York agents, publishers, and writers. I stayed because during those long lunches at Mount Holyoke, Nathan promised to help my career, to help me become a success.

So I stayed while Nathan took off his clothes and sat back down next to me. I let him sit down next to me naked, his chest and arms matted with gray hair that repelled me.

"I promise I won't touch you," he said. "I just want to talk."

Instead, he reran the pornographic film and snorted a few lines of coke and talked about how he often goes to brothels just to talk to the whores about their exploits. He talked about how he goes through his wife's drawers and tries on her underwear. He talked about his dead father.

This went on for nearly two hours. Then finally, he got dressed, took me downstairs, and sent me home in a black limousine that he had called for me, so that I wouldn't have to take the Long Island Railroad. "It's not safe," he said.

"Not safe?" I repeated stupidly, wondering how anything on the train could be more alien or more frightening than what had just happened in this house.

He helped me into the limo. "She'll tell you how to get there," Nathan said to the driver. "Do whatever she says. And charge the trip to my account."

The back seat of the limousine was huge and made of slippery leather that I kept sliding off of whenever the driver made a turn. I felt like a little girl again, like when my parents took me out to dinner at a fine restaurant and even with a phonebook or two underneath me, I still was too small to reach the table. I would sit there in the restaurant chair, swinging my kid-sized feet and very, very quietly take in the world of the grown-ups.

Now I sat in the dark limo listening to the silence. Perhaps this is all a test, a test to see how much I want it—how much I am willing to put up with to make it as a writer. All night, he kept asking me if I thought he was perverted. He wanted me to say no. He needed me to say no. I said I thought he needed someone to talk to.

It is only now in this limo that I know it is I who is perverted. I who stayed and lied to him simply out of ambition.

Tonight is my punishment for Santa Cruz.

DECEMBER 31 (New Year's Eve)

On the way back to the subway today after taking a last-minute dance class in the city, three teenage boys called out to me, "Do you have a nice wide crack? Do you want us to look at your cunt?"

They all laughed.

I clutched my coat tighter to me and walked on. I felt as though the boys had followed me all the way from Santa Cruz.

Why did I remain silent? Why did I not say the words that were within me? What could I say? They wouldn't hear me anyway. They are fourteen, and society has already taught them the power they have. The power to humiliate. To denigrate. To inflict pain.

WINTER

Oh yes, she wanted to live, she loved life, but she also knew that her "I want to live" was spun from the threads of a cobweb. It takes so little, so infinitely little, for a person to cross the border beyond which everything loses meaning: love, convictions, faith, history. Human life—and herein lies its secret—takes place in the immediate proximity of that border, even in direct contact with it; it is not miles away, but a fraction of an inch.

—Milan Kundera, *The Book of Laughter and Forgetting*

JANUARY 4, 1988 (Seattle)

I returned to school to find a mass of bills, my grades, and two rejections of my novel manuscript. Gradewise, I did exceptionally well, two 3.8s in English and a 3.9 in ballet. (Daria soothing her conscience for not casting me in her piece?)

I'm pleased with the grades, though I wonder if I really deserved the high grade that the professor gave me in Early American Lit. He must have really liked my final paper. But it feels good to know that I held my own against the PhD candidates.

Hopefully, this will aid me in getting a teaching assistant position next year, though they say there are only eight positions to go around for both the MFA and PhD programs combined.

And what good is all this if I continue to be rejected by agents and editors? I can't believe I blew off that woman at the Acton Agency two years ago. At twenty-two I had a literary agent, based on the first novel I wrote at Mount Holyoke. At twenty-two all I cared about was dancing, getting into a company. So I didn't keep in touch with her; I didn't tell her I was working on a new book. And when I called the agency a few weeks ago, they told me that she had left to go to law school. They told me that my name wasn't among her files, so that the agency had no record of me. They weren't taking on new clients. It was as though I never existed.

JANUARY 5

I am going to be a good deal busier this quarter than last. My Gender and Mass Culture course requires a lot of heavy reading, much of it theoretical (ugh, literary criticism...).

And while I am only required to write (and rewrite) one short story this quarter, as usual, until I've begun it, I am filled with dread that I will not be able to produce.

Also my aim is to write and write and write, so despite the heavy reading load and my part-time copyediting job, not to mention dance rehearsals twice a week for the winter concert, I've vowed to write no less than three hours a day.

In the spring, I still intend to attempt a play or other live work, though Edgar Rutherford tells me that the Creative Writing Department doesn't offer playwriting. He says if I can get the Theater Department to allow me into its workshops, he'll approve it as a course.

Strange how the university separates all the departments, all the arts. The English Department approves of novels, stories, essays, and poetry. The Theater Department approves of plays. I wonder where you have to go to learn how to write a movie. The School of Communications?

Brad called me on the phone to say he was back from Montana. We were both extremely polite, talked only of theory and philosophy. I didn't ask about the funeral. But it dawned on me suddenly that Brad never states a thought or an idea that he hasn't gotten from some book, as though he is afraid to have any thoughts of his own. Insecure, perhaps, that without textual proof he will not be believed?

Books have had a profound impact on me, especially when I was younger, but lately the only person I find myself quoting is myself. My ideas may not be "official" theory, but I am not necessarily looking for a stated, abstracted definition of life. I'm more interested in the tangible world, messy as it may be.

My body is sore from dance class. It is real and tactile and mine.

JANUARY 7

Tracey called me tonight from Santa Cruz to say she had just gotten married. She actually married that man, that man whose name I dare not utter; she married him on New Year's Eve. She wed him almost at the very instant when those boys were calling out obscenities to me on the New York subway. Boys like that have made similar comments to me throughout most of my adolescence, yet the fact that it upset me more than usual tells me that somehow my body, if not my head, knew, felt deep in my bones, what was taking place on the opposite end of the country.

Tracey married him so he could stay in the U.S. When she told me about marrying that horrible, egomaniacal man, a man who covered my eyes and pinioned my hands behind my back just so he could press his heavy body against me and tell me I was nothing, I went numb.

"Why are you telling me this?" I asked.

"I thought you'd want to know."

"Why?"

"Because we're friends," Tracey said.

"You certainly don't want me to tell you it's all right, do you?"

Silence.

"Because I can't. Because no matter what he may have told you, no matter what you want to believe, I know what happened."

"It's not a real marriage, anyway," Tracey said.

"Pardon?"

"We discussed it and we are both still free to see other people if we want. It's just that this way he won't be deported and I ..."

"What?"

"Well, this way if I meet someone who presses me to date and I don't want to, I can say I'm married. You can't trust the men around here. I'm worried about AIDS."

"I can't even believe what you are saying. I can't believe that I'm listening to this."

"What?"

"Nothing," I said.

But I am thinking about all the men Tracey dated and slept with in college. I am thinking how on the first day I met her, she told me she thought I acted like a stuck-up prig in dance class but then invited me to her room for tea. I am thinking about how she tacked up a giant paper mural on her wall so that whenever I felt afraid or sad I could come in and draw on it. I am thinking about my senior year when one of Tracey's old boyfriends suddenly showed up after five years' absence and how, two weeks later, she came to my room drunk and told me to reserve the following Saturday for a trip to the Northampton courthouse.

"Why?" I asked.

"Because Cass and I are getting married," Tracey said.

Before Tracy had knocked on my door, I had been working on my research paper on Joyce's *Ulysses*. I was analyzing the food imagery in the novel and how what the characters consumed indicated their behavior later in the plot. The task was difficult and rewarding at the same time, and had led me far away from the real world of dorm rooms, boyfriends, and the late hour. So when Tracey announced her engagement in my stark dorm room, I had to blink my eyes a couple of times to focus on what she was saying. Besides, at twenty-one, back at Mount Holyoke after a year off to undergo intensive therapy for depression, I found the concept of marriage as remote as Tracey's journeying to the African bush to live in a house made of dung. But she was giddy from liquor and happiness, and it was hard not to get caught up in her excitement.

"Doesn't Cass live in Texas now?" I said.

"So?"

"What about school? You've still got two years to go."

"Oh bother *school*," Tracey said. "I'm not really good at it like you. Life is more important than school any day. Why read about it when you can live it?"

Such a bold statement made me want to cover up my ears and shut her out, because I felt ashamed that I lacked the courage to tackle life that way. Knowing that about myself, I knew I must support her.

"I would be delighted to stand up at your wedding," I said. "Just tell me the time and place and I'll be there."

The next morning when I asked her if perhaps she wanted to go shopping for a suitable dress, she looked at me as though I were crazy.

"What for?" Tracey asked.

"For the wedding."

"Whose wedding?"

"Yours," I said. "You and Cass."

She laughed, "Oh that. We were just drunk. I mean, we talked about it, but he would drive me nuts. You didn't take me seriously, did you?"

"No," I said, my pride not letting me admit how used I felt. "Of course not."

I am also remembering a year later, after I had already graduated and moved to Boston, how I took the bus back to Mount Holyoke, so that I could sit with her after an abortion. I am thinking about how the following summer she came to share my apartment in Boston and then after a few weeks just drifted away, went back to California. I am thinking about how after she left, the apartment felt too big and quiet and dark, so big and quiet and dark that I gave it up and moved to a smaller place with another friend, so I wouldn't feel alone.

"Listen," I said now over the phone. "I think the marriage will be a disaster. And I realize that as much as I try, I don't hate you."

"That's..." Tracey began.

"I don't hate you, but I can't be involved in your life anymore. As long as you are with him, I don't want to hear from you, know anything about you."

"But..."

I hung up the phone. My hands shook at my daring, for actually saying what I should have said. Forgiveness does not mean you forget. Forgiveness does not mean you shouldn't protect yourself from those who can hurt you.

January 8

I am wary of Anna Rothstein, my new creative writing teacher. She strikes me as a little aphasic. She repeated everything she said in our last class again today. There are only five of us (all women) in the class, two of whom she had as undergraduates. And yet she can't seem to remember our names. How can I trust a woman like that with my own writing?

Yet, at the same time, she strikes me as kind. Truly kind, as though she actually likes students, cares about them. (Sometimes professors do not care for us as people, only as audiences for their egos.) And I'm fascinated by her earlobes, which are the longest I have ever seen. Ears like the Buddha on the front cover of the paperback version of Hesse's *Siddhartha*.

They say she is a science fiction writer, well-known in the genre. Perhaps that is why so few people signed up for her workshop—like me, they are interested in literary fiction, not genre-writing. Yet this was the only short fiction workshop offered this quarter, so here I sit, wary and uncertain and hoping that maybe this quarter I can learn to accept criticism better.

Still my jealousy always interferes. In dance class, I found out that Daria is flying Barbara Mason (a former Mount Holyoke student) in from the East Coast to perform in her piece, rather than cast me. And Karol did not make one comment to me today in rehearsal for the faculty concert.

January 9

Skipped ballet this morning. I am unsure whether it is mere exhaustion or that I just couldn't face Daria's inner circle of dancers. Actually, I've been sad and depressed all day. Santa Cruz and Tracey and confusion about all that has happened these past few months has left me lonely and feeling incredibly lazy and inadequate. Struggling to start the story "Graduation Ball," which explores the relationship between a white dance instructor and her black inner-city students.

Why does my sadness never leave me? Is it because the more I experience the world, the more sadness makes sense? There is true sorrow out there, people living in complete isolation, men and women misunderstanding each other, women distrusting each other and fearing the night.

JANUARY 11

Question: If someone offered you a million dollars to not be depressed, would you stop?

Answer 1: That's like asking a person with a broken leg to run a marathon.

Answer 2: Try me.

Answer 3: Why would anyone ever offer me a million dollars?

JANUARY 12

My mother calls me on the phone. She has heard about Santa Cruz from my sister Linda.

"Linda has a big mouth," I say angrily.

"She thought I should know."

"I asked her not to tell," I say, then silently berate myself, knowing that it is virtually impossible for anyone in my family to keep a secret. It is one of the main reasons I now live three thousand miles away from their well-meaning, highly destructive interference. Coming from a large family is like living out an ongoing game of Telephone: I whisper information about an ailment to one member and by the time it runs through my four sisters, two brothers, and finally lands in my parents' ears, the malady has gone from a minor cut on my hand to congenital heart disease.

"You never tell me anything," my mother says.

"If I didn't want you to know," I said, bracing myself for whatever comes next, "I suppose I wouldn't have told Linda."

She has the opening she needs.

"Well, I'm sure it was difficult for you," she says.

"It would be difficult for anyone."

"Isn't it just possible you misunderstood?"

"Misunderstood what?"

"You know, Sandi," my mother says. "You are a very pretty girl. Maybe you led him to believe you were interested."

My heart begins to pound, my hand begins to feel wet and slippery on the receiver.

"You're saying it is my fault?"

"I'm saying maybe you misunderstood his intentions."

"He blindfolded me, Mother. As far as I know, that is not standard protocol for a seduction."

"How horrible for you."

"Yes, it was, and the last thing I need my mother to do is somehow assert that I am to blame for it."

"I didn't know everything," my mother says.

"So you want to hear it all? You want to hear how he pinned my arms behind my back? About the sound his zipper made when he pulled his penis out of his pants? When I finally got into the dance company in Boston after years of auditions and rejection, you took full credit for it. Do you really want to live this part of my life for me as well?"

"That's unfair," my mother says, softly.

"It certainly is," I say and hang up.

But it is too late. Even though I know I am right and my mother wrong, the seed of doubt that has been slowly germinating in my mind has now been planted. Maybe I had blown the assault out of proportion. After all, he didn't really rape me. But then, why do I still feel so violated? Why do I jump at every strange noise I hear? The uncertainty hangs around me like a gang of hooligans keeping watch on a street corner. Malevolent and omnipresent.

JANUARY 13

Myth: It rains all the time in Seattle.

Fact: It does not so much rain as spit. Just now, the spit falls mean-spiritedly, landing with a cold clammy plop on the exposed parts of my body. Hands, the back of the neck, the rounded part of my forehead where it trickles down my face to annoy my left ear. Yet when I examine my raincoat, there is no trace of raindrops, no tiny balled-up beads of moisture.

I look up at the overcast skies, skies that often remain gray for days, even weeks at a time, seeking to find the being that resides up beyond those darkened clouds. I rarely think of God, generally am confident of his noninterference in the lives of us mortals, but the way the rain falls here seems so much like the old vaudevillian gag of seltzer spritzing in your face, that some higher form of intelligence must be causing it all.

After leaving two umbrellas behind at various places on campus in early November, I've long since given up carrying one to protect myself. There seems little point, for the moment I pop up the top, the rain stops. I take it down, the drops fall. Some Groucho Marx of the skies is up there laughing his head off.

JANUARY 14

Brad called me again tonight. We went to see *Broadcast News*. We went with two of his friends, a married couple, Dan and Callie, who also brought their baby. This is the first time Brad has introduced me to the other people in his life, which must mean he has finally called it quits with Juleen, though of course pride keeps me from asking.

It was funny watching Brad with a baby. He seems very into the kid and the idea of having a kid. He kept asking Callie and Dan questions about the baby's development.

I was far more interested in watching him than the infant. In the old stereotypes, women are supposed to go ga-ga about babies, not the men.

Afterwards, Brad walked me to my door while his friends waited in the car. We both stared at each other a few minutes and knew that there was no longer anything between us. We had been drawn to each other sexually, but our minds never seem to meet, running perpetually in parallel lines that can't ever cross. And I simply no longer have the energy to try to make him love me.

So we shook hands, wished each other luck, and that was the end of Brad Baldwin in my life.

JANUARY 16

I heard—yes, on a television commercial—that people supposedly read a thousand books in their lifetime. I assume that if I haven't yet reached that number, I will shortly have done so. I've decided to record the date and title of every book I read after I finish it. Perhaps to keep track of my next thousand, but more to be able to see *what* I am reading, to track how my feelings about books and writing change.

Anyway, I just finished *Brothers in Arms* by William Broyles Jr. for my Gender and Mass Culture class. Non-fiction. Non-moving. I know the guy comes from a journalistic background, but I thought, as a Vietnam vet, he would be more in touch with the subject he writes about. He supposedly goes back to Vietnam ten years after the war to reface his "enemy," to come to know Vietnam and its people. That's what he said his goal was in the book's preface. But basically all I see him doing is trying to find excuses. Oh, he accepts the "blame" of the American government in the war and, unlike Ronald Reagan, he knows that the U.S. lost, but in fact this is what he keeps harping on over and over again. That we lost. And why we lost.

But he never really does come to know the Vietnamese. I think he marvels at them as if they were animals at the zoo, even admires them for being "fighting machines," people who never give up, always going after what they wanted—their country back—but I think it is this very admiration that keeps him from seeing them as individuals and people.

Of course the Vietnamese fought hard—it's their land, just as we beat the British despite being outnumbered during the Revolutionary War. And even though I know many of the U.S. soldiers who fought and died there were, as Broyles puts it, "victims of the American government and society—uneducated, often black, always poor," I still feel greater compassion for the Vietnamese than I do for the American soldiers.

Perhaps I have no right to judge. I have never been a soldier, never been in or even witnessed a war or battle, and perhaps my prejudices against the military in general get in my way. But I think the real reason we get involved in wars in the first place is because if we win we can feel good about ourselves, drop all the difficult problems we can't solve, like pollution and poverty and racism, and rally behind a single issue—like rooting for a football game. The only way to stop war is for both fans and players to refuse to show up for the game.

January 21

My Gender and Mass Culture class is a huge disappointment.

I sit there every week completely confused by the words they toss around: words like "polemics," "objectification," and "hegemony" (which I have to keep looking up because every time I feel I have a true grasp of its meaning, a student uses the word in a different way and tries to apply it to a totally different situation). Terms and ideas thrown out at me as though the key to a complicated puzzle. But do all these theories, these buzz words, really bring us closer to human understanding? Do they not, instead, serve to distance us even further from our subject, our own humanity, simply because we are so caught up in the language of definition, of positing and suppositions that we fail to clue in to what is "actually" happening?

I thought things would improve this week because the class was to discuss Didion's novel *Democracy*. It was the real reason I signed up for the class in the first place. I have read everything Joan Didion has written so far (at least twice), yet always on my own, so I was looking forward to discussing it in class.

But all the students seemed interested in was deciding whether or not Didion's writing supported the dominant patriarchy. They argued it did, because even though the protagonist, Inez Victor, does eventually leave her emotionally abusive husband, she runs into the arms of another man. One woman thought this showed that Joan Didion felt that a woman could not be whole without a man, any man, in her life.

I am outraged. "Maybe she simply ran away with Jack Lovett," I said, "because she has been in love with him since she was sixteen years old."

En masse, the class turned to look at me.

"What do you mean?" Justine Clark, our professor, prompted.

"Women fall in love with men," I said. "It happens all the time. The tragedy of the story is that Inez followed convention for so long that when she finally did get to be with Jack after twenty years, he dies almost immediately of a heart attack."

"But whose theory are you basing that on?" another woman asked me.

"I beg your pardon?" I asked, stunned.

"Theory? Where are you getting your ideas from?"

"There's no theory. It's just my opinion. Women leave men for other lovers all the time. It's real. People move from one place to another, from one person to another. It's what happens in life *and* narrative."

There was silence.

No one talked to me for the rest of the hour.

January 23

Today in my Gender and Mass Culture class, we talked about Guy Dubord's *Society of the Spectacle,* and about the concept of "authentic experience." The class debated whether it was possible to have one, since the immediacy of the media automatically turns individual events into a shared spectacle.

It never occurred to me that it wasn't possible.

What's with these people?

January 26

What's with me that I care what these people think? Just finished writing a three-page report on *Male Fantasies,* which, among other things, explores the sexual and violent dreams, books, and artwork that the Freicorps (proto-Nazis) experienced. In the book, the author Klaus Theweleit argues that these proto-Nazis fundamentally feared women, thus both vilifying and deifying women at the same time. Using German literature and advertising from the early 1920s, he demonstrates how in these men's emotional lives, women appeared in only two ways: as the White Nurse or Nun, a sexless, benevolent creature who comforts men with a cool hand and nourishing food; or as the Red Rifle Woman, an insatiable killer whose sole aim in life is to swallow up a man whole. Drawing on Freudian dream imagery, Theweleit discusses how these early Nazis associated anything red with the menstrual cycle, which is why they had such an omnipresent hatred and fear of the Communist Party.

It seems like a huge jump when I present it here, but after eight hundred pages of examples and pictures and analysis, some of Theweleit's theory makes sense, which is why the book disturbed me so. Even though he uses these Freicorps soldiers as the model, I couldn't help applying it to some of the men in power today.

The hardest part of the assignment is to summarize the main points of the book in three pages. (How can you raise such complex issues in just three pages and expect any kind of real discussion?)

I worry about how my paper will be received by Clark and her students. I worry they will laugh at me or give me that cold, cold silence. Why do I care about impressing Clark when I don't really respect what she teaches?

Actually, I think what she has to say is interesting; it's some of the *students* who really bug me. Like any new convert to a religion or teaching, their commitment to "feminist" theory borders on fanaticism, a practice which can be just as damaging to women as male domination.

Still, I want to impress Justine Clark with my intelligence, because (like Daria) she is a woman with authority, respect, and someone who inspires others.

Or maybe I just don't want to be invisible in that class anymore.

As for my real work, my writing, Anna Rothstein has looked at my novel. She said she wasn't the best person to evaluate the book because it reminded her too much of her own Jewish, New York upbringing. I've decided to take that statement as a compliment, in that I've obviously managed to create a true sense of place in the book. Anna also says that I am not a short-story writer at heart—that my true writer's self is to be found in novels.

I'm not sure what to make of that, except that I know that character is what I care about. Characters who change and grow and interact with others. Short stories don't really give one enough time to do characterization—they are more concerned about one particular event than in psychological portraiture.

They are also about description. While description itself really comes rather easily to me, I often stumble when I try to use it to advance plot. Writing, like dancing, is about movement; but my work always feels stifled—a picture of a dancer doing an arabesque, not the arabesque itself.

As for my depression, I keep telling myself that I must work through it. I think it is simply a matter of keeping busy, of putting projects before me, projects and goals like submitting my application for the Milliman Prize, a $5,000 scholarship that they award to only one writing student per year. Of course I want to win it—not only for the money. I want to win it because of what it will say about the winner. That she has talent. Ability.

I am too competitive. I am too competitive. I am too competitive!

JANUARY 27

Before I left Boston, my therapist suggested that it might help me settle in faster if I could see someone out here.

"That way you won't have to go it alone," Gloria said.

So now I have a Seattle therapist named Dr. Lane. She is a newly minted graduate of the UW Medical School, finishing up her residency in psychiatry.

She has short, serious dark hair that lies flat against her head, as though a stray flyaway would not dare interfere with the task at hand. She is utterly humorless, probably because they stress distance in medical school—to keep a cool, objective wall between the doctor and the crazy patient.

When I look at Dr. Lane, I think longingly of Gloria back in her pastel-decorated Cambridge office. She always had boxes of tissues strewn unobtrusively about, so wherever I sat and suddenly began crying there was always a soft Kleenex to bury my nose into. Dr. Lane also keeps tissues in her office, but only one box, hospital stock, that she's placed right on her desk. That means I have to be composed enough to get up and actually cross the room.

Dr. Lane frowns on crying; it interferes with the work we are doing. Sometimes I wish Dr. Lane would tell me exactly what work it is that we are trying to accomplish. Sometimes I want to ask Dr. Lane if maybe it would just be easier to have her analyze me without my being there.

I do not like Dr. Lane, but if I want to continue receiving treatment at the university clinic for a modest twelve dollars an hour, either it is she or I go it alone. It is not that I am proud of needing someone to talk to about my problems, but after being in and out of therapy for the past six years, I no longer see it as a sign of weakness, a flaw in my character.

Still, the university hides us away. To get to Dr. Lane's office, I must journey down the Burke-Gilman trail to a square, plain, barely adequate building covered in gray-and-white stucco. Unlike the other campus buildings, which proudly display their names in big bold lettering, this building simply has a sign that says "Property of the University of Washington" and a number. If any place could make a person feel anonymous and isolated in a confusing world, this building would do it. When I open the heavy gray door, I feel like a pervert dressed in a trench coat who feels the need to expose himself every week.

Perhaps that is why, when I get really bored with Dr. Lane, I tell her lies.

I tell her that Daria George is my real mother who gave me up for adoption, and that the real reason she never casts me in any of her dance pieces is because she doesn't want to show favoritism.

I tell her that I don't have a uterus so I can't give birth.

I tell her that my professor Justine Clark has a God-complex and that I am one of the fallen angels cast out from female heaven.

I tell her that I used to have anorexia nervosa and that sometimes I still go without eating for days at a time. (What I don't tell her, for then I fear she really will think I am sick, is that I used to fantasize about being anorectic, because in my sixteen-year-old mind I thought anorexia would make me a more interesting person.)

I recite the first two paragraphs of my Pulitzer Prize acceptance speech.

I do not talk about Santa Cruz or my mother's phone calls accusing me of tempting men. I do not tell her how all month long I've been plagued by writer's block.

Dr. Lane is disgusted with me—I can see that by the way she takes notes, concentrating hard on each word as she writes. A long furrow runs across her forehead.

I am a belligerent patient but feel only slightly guilty about the way I treat her.

Lying feels good. It gives me some semblance of control.

JANUARY 30

When I came home from photocopying my stories for the Milliman Prize application, I found a strange man in our apartment. One of us must have left the door open by mistake, because I cannot think how else he could have gotten in.

Anyway, I walked into the living room and there he was—a tall, thin, nearly emaciated black man wandering around. "Can I help you?" I said, thinking maybe he was a friend of one of my suitemates.

Suddenly, he puts his arms up over his head, as if I had turned a gun on him. I suppose he was as surprised as I was to see someone there.

"I'm looking for the rental office, lady," he said.

"The university owns the building," I said. "But the housing office is at least three blocks away. Why are you *really* here?"

"I told you, lady."

"I think you should leave."

"I didn't take anything," he said, suddenly. "You can frisk me if you want. Didn't take a thing."

And he backed out of the apartment, still holding up his hands.

The whole thing happened so fast that it never occurred to me to be afraid. He was in our apartment, and I wanted him to leave; he intruded upon my life. It is only afterwards that I realize I am more furious than I am scared. Perhaps because I knew that at least this time I did have some control. Perhaps because I am tired of trying to find a way to justify Santa Cruz, when there is no way to justify it. Perhaps because when our bodies are at stake, we feel fear, but when only our material goods are at risk, we feel anger. I don't know how long the intruder was here, but I am sure that he had the chance to see the new computer my father bought me so I wouldn't have to walk home from the computer lab on campus late at night.

We all went through our rooms carefully. The only thing he managed to steal was a favorite box of Alda's, which contained a few dimes and quarters. We reported the incident to campus security, but they didn't think there was much they could do. (We all vowed to lock the front door consistently from now on.)

Perhaps I should have been nastier when I asked him to leave, more suspicious, but he acted so strange, so frightened of me that I wanted to give him the benefit of the doubt. Or perhaps I wanted to show him that I was not suspicious of him simply because of his color. None of this was conscious, of course. It is only now, reflecting back on it, that I recognize what I was doing.

Did he perhaps sense this in me, my middle-class morality, my white self trying desperately not to be aware of its whiteness? Did he sense this and play upon my innate guilt, and thus easily escape without my calling the police or asking him to account for himself? All I said was "Leave. Go right now."

I have become so aware of my "whiteness" lately; prejudices I did not think I had are surfacing but in an odd way. I go out of my way to make excuses for racial minorities, to want not to believe all the stereotypes this country has created for them. But my prejudice stems from the knowledge that I am *deliberately* trying not to see their color, and in so doing I wind up seeing it more.

Who am I really furious at ... the intruder or myself?

I've begun reading *The Diary of Anais Nin* (Vol. I), a used copy which I found at the Magus bookstore. If I believed in Hinduism or reincarnation or something, I would like to think that I was Nin in a previous life. (For purposes of my fantasy, I will ignore the fact that she was still alive when I was born.)

Her journal entries are like novels, metaphors and descriptions clean and neat. She lived a life of emotion, of richness, absorbed in the half-passion and complexities of feeling, of inwardness. And yes, for a time, she was a dancer.

But what would it be like to live in Paris? Would things look differently to me there?

Nin writes about her naiveté, her innocence despite the "artistic" life she supposedly led. I too am naive. Yet I cannot help being drawn to that which is not naive, to those people, those men who are slightly dangerous, who carry their hurts and rages and lies not on their faces, but in their words and actions. It's like I'm a "danger" junkie; I both fear and love my need for such men in my life.

I'm thinking about Anais Nin and Henry Miller when I write this. I see her attraction to him, just as I see how it will turn out, the way it turned out for me and Nathan Katz a few months ago. The way it turned out for me and Brad.

If Anais Nin and I had met, would we have liked each other? Or in my envy, would I have turned away and not dared to really see her, the way I can see her in her diaries?

Was she at all aware (she must have been aware) when she was writing that someday others might look at her words? Did she ever feel self-conscious about them, concerned about an invisible audience, as I so often am?

FEBRUARY 1 (4 a.m.)

I cannot put Nin's *Diary* down. And when I do take a break, it is only so that I may write here about its significance for me. Reading it makes me feel both sad and glad, sad because I realize that now there is no longer a need for my own work because a beautiful woman fifty years ago has already said what I want to say, and she does so magnificently. My writing is crude by comparison. Yet glad, too, because now I know that I am not alone in my thought, my isolation isn't as complete.

I must be careful, very careful, not to make a complete equation (emotionally) between her and myself. That could be dangerous, disastrous.

And I wonder what do fifty years, a different country, and a nuclear bomb have to do with the differences between us? And her amazing talent.

I do not want to say that Nin speaks for all women or that she is Woman (this is what those students do in my Mass Culture class), but that she reaches not the woman in me but my femaleness.

She writes of her lack of confidence. Yet how strong she is, how unafraid she is to admit that her work is good, that she has talent, a sense of who she is.

How I would like to admit these things without feeling guilty of vanity or egotism. I would be so tremendously relieved if I could be strong within myself, be sure of my talent. Not so much as "dancer" or "writer" but as an artist; to allow myself to admit this without anticipating jeers, cries of "snob," "elitist," etc.

Why is this so hard to do? Why is it that even now I am battling with my psyche in order to admit such a thing aloud?

When I was nineteen and thought about killing myself, my parents sent me to a therapist who was a friend of a friend. She was an older woman, and I liked her, but I always felt my parents had told her to make me give up my dancing career; they thought it was my desire to dance that made me want to die.

Perhaps on the surface they were right, though only superficially. It was the fear that I would never be good enough, not only as a dancer but as human being, that I would always fail simply because I am so afraid of living. Dancing was my dream, because I thought if I could conquer that world, if Daria believed I was good enough to dance on the stage, Daria who never lied to me, then I could conquer life itself.

But I remember this therapist telling me to wake every morning and say "I am not a dancer" twenty times aloud. "If you say it often enough," she said, "it will no longer feel so painful." Then she told me I should say "I am a human being" twenty times. I say it now.

"Nothing," I still hear his voice hiss inside me. "Say you are nothing."

FEBRUARY 2

Began reading *Take Back the Night,* a series of essays on pornography, for my Mass Culture class. I've become fascinated with men's fascination with pornography, with the innate violence that seems to accompany it.

It is hard to read the book because my heart says one thing about the topic, my upbringing another, and logic yet another. And while certainly I believe some pornography clearly denigrates women, as a writer I worry about the concept of censorship.

Yet does my work help keep the myth going, help promote a man's violent treatment of a woman simply because I often write about individuals who are drawn to dangerous men?

People say that pornography is the ugly side of sexuality, but it seems so entrenched in societal values, in religious ideology and political rhetoric that I don't think it's about sexuality at all. My sexuality is mine, the person inside who wants to be loving and beautiful and passionate, who wants to give of herself, but more than that—wants to be given to.

Still, I am afraid. I am a woman and I am put upon, hurt, raped because of this fact. And I don't want to be afraid anymore. I want the world to be better, to change its dangerous values, yet won't that happen not by silencing men, but by giving women more of a voice?

FEBRUARY 3

Read more of Nin's *Diary*. Her father, a famous pianist, said that the two most horrible men to ever live were Jesus Christ and Columbus—Jesus because he introduced guilt and Columbus because he "discovered" America and materialism.

I do not know what to think of that. But I do think of all the American artists in exile. Josephine Baker, Fitzgerald, Hemingway, Stein, Anais Nin, Henry Miller. The countless Americans who have gone off to Europe to dance, to write, to create. And myself and my dream of traveling to Italy. Why is it that we have to leave America to write, and yet remain so distinctly American? Or do we?

I know, whether good or bad, that I am an American, have American values and American sensibilities. And yet I am so very critical of this country, of its hypocrisy, of its ugliness, its blindness, its inability to apprehend Art, the necessity of Art. Politicians and bureaucrats love to espouse freedom, and yet it is a specific, very closed sort of freedom they talk about.

I feel so caught up in a bind, torn between my inner artistic self and my complete submersion into American mass culture, including graduate school.

FEBRUARY 8

Read the last part of Nin's *Diary*. She discusses Dr. Otto Rank and his perceptions of women, neurosis, and Art. He argues that a neurotic woman becomes an artist out of need; once she is cured of her neuroses, she becomes a complete woman and no longer desires to create.

How could Nin accept this without balking? She seems to accept that she is an artist because she is a "failed" woman, that because she finds it difficult to love only one man (she is married and having an affair with Henry Miller), therefore she needs art.

This is an absurd concept. I think that artists, writers, dancers, etc., are very interested in people or in their environment or in history or in a hundred other things; their restlessness stems not from neurosis, but simply from feeling life strongly and wanting to feel more and yet more. The sidebars, loneliness and sorrow, are not the sole domain of artists; if that were true, then three-quarters of the population would be writing books or painting canvases this very minute.

What troubles me even more, however, is Dr. Rank's supposition that it is men who created the Soul. He argues that women see reality for what it is and therefore do not need the inwardness of the soul.

Why didn't Nin challenge him? How could she swallow whole what Rank said? Is it merely because it was fifty years ago and she, herself, was not yet aware of the implicit sexism behind his analysis?

I suddenly hate myself for noticing this and the blatant sexism in film, TV, and the media. Yes, this Gender and Mass Culture class is raising my consciousness, but in an ugly way. It robs me of the things I enjoy; still worse, it is so clinical, almost blinding in its own ideology. I suddenly find myself unable to look at or view anything without its having a gender significance, without attaching the question of gender to it.

I know this is what the activists desire, and certainly without the feminist movement, I too might have been forced to buy into Rank's theories, but the constant, endless looking for the ways in which men denigrate women also seems wrong to me somehow— dehumanizing, and therefore dangerous.

I suppose I can't truly believe in Causes. I only believe in the individuals who make up or serve a Cause.

Four years at a women's college taught me about possibility, about the limitless potential of women, of people, of myself. It taught me without indoctrinating me in ideology, taught me simply because two thousand women were there with me—living, doing, working towards the challenge of themselves.

FEBRUARY 9

Today one of the women in my writing class (her name is Felicia Phillips) invited all of us to a birthday party she was throwing for her husband. I found this invitation strange since none of us have met her husband, none of us really know her, but mostly because I am still stunned when people my age are married.

When I was a little girl I thought that the day after your nineteenth birthday, you fell off the earth. My eight-year-old mind simply couldn't fathom an age older than that. I mean, I knew my parents were old, but they were my parents and, as such, not real people. Although I did have older brothers and sisters, and thus understood the concept of being fifteen or sixteen years old, I couldn't imagine much more beyond that. My siblings seemed so different from me, their interests so removed from mine, and I was always being told that the difference had to do with being older.

"Why can't I go with them?" I might ask my mother.

"Because they are older," she would reply.

And, of course, at parties there was the kids' table, where my little sister Linda and I were always put (no matter how old I got, the cutoff point for leaving that table always seemed to be exactly one year more than I was), while my other siblings got to sit with the grown-ups.

When my brother Dave turned thirteen, he was bar mitzvahed. When Eileen and Jenny turned sixteen, they had a Sweet Sixteen party. But after that, there seemed to be nothing. As my brothers and sisters grew older, I would see them less and less, returning home after I was already in bed. They would flit in and out of the house like giant butterflies, pausing only long enough to alight on a chair for a meal or exchange their old blue-jean-clad skin for a more colorful red miniskirt. My eldest brother, Peter, left for college when I was eleven, and four years later when he came back, he did so only to pick up the rest of his belongings and move on.

Perhaps my uncertainty about what lay beyond childhood had to do with going away to college. As long as I could remember, my parents spoke of college as a magical place, a place where you were transformed, became wise, became special. And so I eagerly awaited the day when I, too, could leave for this place; I could leave behind everything about me I didn't want people to know about, including my difficult childhood, and begin anew.

At college, four weeks before my nineteenth birthday, I attempted suicide by swallowing a handful of sleeping pills. The immediate cause was that Daria had once more decided not to cast me in the spring dance concert, but even before all the shrinks and doctors began crawling around in my head, I think I knew it was much more than my failure as a dancer. I was still waiting for that transformation, that miraculous moment when I felt wiser, a better person than the one I thought I was at eight or twelve or sixteen. I guess I foolishly thought that by killing myself, I would freeze time, still be the emerging pupa, not the failed butterfly. I think I must have realized just how foolish a thought it was, because less than two minutes after I ingested the pills, I threw them back up. Ten minutes after that, deeply angry at myself, my limbs shaking from fear, I ran the half-mile to Daria's office and told her what I had just done. Then I passed out in her arms. When I came to, I was in the college infirmary. While the medical staff waited for the on-call shrink to drive to the college to evaluate me, a nurse's aid sat next to my bed to make sure that I remained calm.

"Do you want to talk with a priest, honey?" the woman asked.

Even as confused as I was, I remember rolling my eyes at so absurd a suggestion. "I don't need God," I said. "I just need better feet."

Now I have lived nearly five years past that date. Now I see myself as only five years old, the person I became when I finally accepted that non-transformation was the standard mode of living for most human beings. The person I am now, who still remains chronically disappointed that wisdom (and thus happiness) doesn't just come to you because a certain birthday passes.

Why am I writing all this?

Because when I look at Felicia Phillips, I see that same chronic disappointment in her eyes. It is too painful to see it in someone else, to have it staring back at me whenever I speak to her. So I lied. I told her I would be delighted to come. But even as I said it, I knew that I had absolutely no intention of showing up.

FEBRUARY 13

I went. I couldn't *not* go, because half an hour after the party was scheduled to begin, I received a phone call from Marianne Smithson, who is another student in our writing class.

"I'm the only one here," she said to me quietly over the phone.

"Where?" I said.

"At Felicia's."

"What do you mean? She told me she invited everyone in the program. And her science fiction friends. Like twenty or thirty people."

"They didn't come," Marianne said.

"Oh God," I said.

In my mind, I picture Felicia's already disappointed eyes growing hard and shiny with panic.

"I'll be right over," I said.

"Hurry," Marianne said.

So I ran a brush quickly through my thick hair, stuck a pony-tail holder around it, grabbed my purse, and was on my way.

I took a Number 70 bus to Eastlake Avenue, where Felicia and her husband, John, lived in an apartment in a large purple-and-white building. At the entry, I was greeted by the thick dank smell of rotten burnt cabbage, the smell of poverty and neglect, of one-pot dinners cooked too quickly on small inadequate stoves that either burn too hot or burn not at all. It is the same smell that emanated from my grandmother's apartment about a month before her death.

My pace slowed as I climbed the three flights of stairs to Felicia's apartment (stairs that wrap around the outside of the building so everyone from the street can watch you ascend), frightened by what I might find.

I knocked on Felicia's metal door.

Felicia opened it quickly.

"Sandi!" and she threw her arms around me in a tight hug.

I felt her thin body through her blue cotton sweater. I am used to being around ninety-pound girlwomen, but Felicia's body lacks the taut, well-developed muscles of a dancer. All I felt was bone. As she wrapped those tiny arms around me, I had a terrifying image of my aunt wasting away in her cancer bed, her skeleton eyes boring into mine.

I did not hug Felicia back.

I looked across the room, where Marianne sat on an over-stuffed flowered sofa.

She smiled at me; it was the warmest thing in the place.

"This is my husband, John," Felicia said, bringing her husband over to me.

I shook his hand.

"Happy Birthday," I said and handed him a card that I had luckily bought a few weeks early for Rachel's birthday and thus had lying around my room.

"Yeah, thanks," he said.

John looked like a muppet. The one on *Sesame Street* known as "The Count," with a soft spongy head, fanged eyeteeth, a slit for a mouth, and a Dracula cape. John had it all but the cape.

But Felicia looked at him like he was God. "John writes too," she said.

"So you're in the program?" I asked. "Is that how you met?"

"Nah," John said. "Never finished high school."

"Oh," I said. I have never met a person our age who failed to complete high school.

"But he's working on his GED—right, honey?" Felicia said.

"Yeah," John said.

"So, what do you write?" I asked, feeling this would be safer ground.

"Science fiction stuff like Felicia. About the government conspiracy to take away our rights."

"Which conspiracy is that?" I asked, feeling a tightening in my chest, thinking of Santa Cruz.

"Well, for God's sake, look at this place. Artists just aren't valued in the United States. We have to slave all day long just to find some time to create after work."

"It makes me mad, too," I said. "But I'm hoping that if I can land a teaching job at a college, that will free up my time to write."

"I know a really talented poet who drives a Metro bus," Marianne said. "He makes a lot of money driving and can do it part-time."

"So what slave labor do you do, John?" I asked, jokingly.

"Actually, he's between jobs," Felicia said.

"Oh," I said again, once more taking in the sparseness of the room.

On the stove, a single pot of spaghetti boiled. John and Felicia are just one step away from burnt rotten cabbage.

"Felicia's in school and you're out of work, how do you guys live?"

"I do typing for some of the professors on campus," Felicia said. "And we get help from Jewish Family Services downtown."

"I didn't know you were Jewish," I said.

"John's not," Felicia said. "I knew that Jews were really into families and were very supportive. So I converted about a year ago."

"You became a Jew because they give out the best welfare?" I asked.

"We've got to live somehow," John said.

"That's not the only reason," Felicia said. "I find it a very interesting religion."

"But you can't just become a Jew," I said. "There is a very strict conversion process."

"Yeah," Felicia said. "It was cool. I studied with this rabbi for a while and I had to go through this long bath ritual."

"The *mikvah*," I said.

"Right," Felicia said. "These women helped me undress and then I had to be dunked in this milky water over and over again."

Growing up, I had heard the story of my father's Hungarian cousin Sandor, who somehow miraculously managed to escape from a Nazi concentration camp. After several years as a refugee, he finally wound up in America. As soon as he got here, he converted to Christianity, wanting to leave all aspects of his former life behind. Given that the Jews have suffered two thousand years of persecution, I could understand Sandor's decision (though to paraphrase Gertrude Stein, Sandor of all people should know that a Jew is a Jew is a Jew). But I could not understand a person going the other way simply because of a well-organized charity program.

"I need to sit down," I said, and plopped down next to Marianne on the flowered couch. The added weight squeezed a piece of white stuffing out of a hole in the upholstery like a cottony fart.

"I feel guilty eating here," I whispered to Marianne. "Maybe we should offer to go get them something."

"Good idea," Marianne said. "I'll go with you."

"That spaghetti could probably use some bread," I said carefully. "Why don't we just go pick some up? It's only fair that we contribute some food."

Marianne and I quickly let ourselves out of the apartment and walked down to a small overpriced grocery on the corner.

"She can't be for real," I said.

"They are a bit odd," Marianne said.

I looked over at Marianne. Her pretty, polite, blonde appearance, her sweet manner and good sense of humor, completely belie her dead seriousness about her writing. In class, I always find her comments about my work to be accurate and useful, which has made me trust her.

Suddenly, we both burst out laughing. We laughed because Felicia and John's situation is so pathetic. We laughed because if we did not, we would cry.

We laughed together, and I realized that I have finally made a friend in Seattle. Once I recognized that, she and I talked easily, not only about Felicia but about ourselves and our fears and hopes. We purchased the bread and a liter of soda, and journeyed back to Felicia's place.

The rest of the evening went pretty much like any small standard birthday celebration, though Marianne and I both ate sparingly and there still was barely enough to go around. And when Felicia brought the sugary-sweet birthday cake to the table, it was already half-eaten and stale.

"One of the ladies at Hadassah gave it to me," Felicia said. "It was left over from some function. A perfectly good cake going to waste."

As soon as I got back to my apartment, I ran for my bank book to confirm I still owned cash. There is one hundred and fifteen dollars left in my checking account until payday, but in my entire life I have never had to eat donated leftovers.

I feel the shame of the survivor.

FEBRUARY 15

Had a dream last night about Nathan Katz. While set in New York, I knew all the action took place in the future (though Nathan and I were the ages we are now) since the images of the city were of a damp, dark and deserted place. In fact, the only life that seemed to exist was at Nathan's apartment.

I dropped in on him—I was no longer a New Yorker—perhaps passing through to somewhere else. We talked a while, and then Nathan said I should join in on a secret meeting being conducted in his basement (because it is a dream I guess it is possible that an apartment on 92nd Street could have a basement).

At the meeting were a group of young people, eighteen or nineteen years old, one representing each of the seven continents. They were all gathering together to form an alliance of some sort, but one I sensed was vaguely militaristic and violence-oriented, like in *Road Warrior*.

So I left the group and came back upstairs to Nathan's kitchen, where a beautiful Asian woman sat. Nathan held onto her hand and kept telling her, impressing upon her, his intellect, his artistry, his manhood.

I watched him and felt angry, angry because he was going to hurt this young woman, because she would believe in him blindly like I once did. My admiration had turned to disgust. I told him so.

So we fought in front of this beautiful Asian woman, and I found myself yelling all the things I truly feel inside about him, that he is weak, that his obsession with pornography is hurtful, that he never truly saw me as me, just this image he had created in his mind, that he was a fraud—a phony.

Then suddenly Nathan turned into the man from Santa Cruz.

I woke up screaming.

FEBRUARY 15 (Later the Same Day)

Dr. Lane was in a foul mood. I think she finally has caught on about all the lies I've been telling her. She said that therapy could only help if I was honest with her. So then I tell Dr. Lane everything. I tell her about Santa Cruz, and Tracey's decision to get married, and Nathan's love of pornography, and my mother's accusations. I tell it to her like a story, thinking if I tell it like a story it won't be as real. I don't talk about how I feel. I close my eyes, turn away from Dr. Lane, and give her narrative. Lots and lots of narrative.

"Oh, Sandi, I'm so glad you've come," Tracey says to me, stretching her hands over her head in a generous movement that seems to take in the whole world. "We'll have such great fun now that you are here."

I smile at her, relieved to know that Tracey is exactly the same as I remembered her. Exactly as though three years haven't passed since we have last seen each other.

We sit on Tracey's sofa drinking white wine and talking, listening to the salty breezes from the night ocean sweep through the open patio doors.

After Tracey had picked me up from the airport in San Francisco, we had Thanksgiving dinner at Tracey's uncle's house. It was awkward and uncomfortable celebrating the holiday with strangers, especially when Tracey told me that she only saw these people maybe once every five years. By the time we drive to Tracey's condo in Santa Cruz, the strain of meeting new people had given me a splitting headache.

But we change into comfortable clothing and I sit down on the couch. Tracey stands barefoot by the open patio doors, the wind pulling at her white terry robe.

"See, Snatty," Tracey says, using her pet name for me, and joining me on the couch. "It is November, but we are not shut up tightly in the house in Boston or Seattle, checking to see if the old heater has run out of oil. This is California, baby. Here everyone is well."

I look at Tracey's tanned skin, her Rubenesque body, and agree that, yes, she does indeed look well. Even the way Tracey smokes her French cigarettes seems healthy, carefree, for she does not puff away like a compulsive addict, merely takes deep, periodic drags. Most of the time, she just lets the cigarette burn down in her left hand, the smoke spiraling up to the ceiling of the darkened room.

The cigarettes, like the freshly frosted ribbon of blonde in Tracey's hair, are new additions to her lexicon, her vast vocabulary of body language of which she is so clearly, so uninhibitedly, proud. I am back with one of my closest friends, back with someone whom I don't have to impress with my writing skills or my great insights into literature. I am here with Tracey. I am safe.

The phone rings.

Tracey sets down her wine glass on the coffee table and reaches for the receiver. "Hello? Eduardo!"

Suddenly, I feel transported halfway around the world, for Tracey is now talking rapidly in Spanish. Tracey is a language wizard. She grew up in the last town on California's southern border and spent a good deal of her childhood in Mexico. She speaks Spanish flawlessly. In college, she added both Italian and Portuguese to her repertoire.

"That was Eduardo," she says, hanging up the phone.

"Who is Eduardo?"

"I told you, Sandi. I told you all about him in my last letter. Don't you remember?"

"You tell me about a lot of people in your letters, Tracey."

"Oh, but not Eduardo, he's special."

I look at Tracey skeptically. She has never called any man special before. In fact, one of the things I most admire about Tracey is her ability to not only collect men the same way other people collect socks, but also to discard them just as coolly, as unsentimentally, as if the men themselves had simply worn out.

"What's so special about him?"

"Everything. He's Argentinian. Comes from this wealthy family, a ranch owner or something. Only Eduardo hates his father and got into politics. He's a leftist. A socialist. He's come to the United States to try to get a better understanding of how capitalism works, so he can then go back and overthrow the government."

"I didn't know anyone wanted to overthrow the Argentine government. Isn't that one of the more stable countries?"

"Somebody always wants to overthrow a government, Sandi. It's the only way to achieve change in South America. Don't you follow what's going on down there?"

"Tracey, I barely follow what's going on here. Apart from attending an antinuclear rally with my brother when I was twelve years old, and signing all those petitions protesting apartheid in college, I'm hardly what you would call politically active. I've never even met a revolutionary before."

Tracey laughs.

"So Eduardo studies economics at UC-Santa Cruz?"

Tracey shakes her head impatiently. "No, dummy, he washes dishes at the El Paso."

"El Paso?"

"It's a restaurant. He's not here legally, you know. He's on a tourist visa. So he washes dishes to make money. I told him we'd pick him up at the restaurant. He gets off work in an hour."

"Why doesn't he just get a regular visa?"

"Would you give a visa to someone whose main intention is to overthrow a federal republic? Of course, he says he may not do that. He may just open an import/export business instead."

I laugh.

"What's so funny?"

"Nothing, Tracey. It is just so good to see you again."

Tracey smiles. "C'mon downstairs and you can unpack. I've got to go dress before we pick Eduardo up."

The restaurant is in the middle of nowhere, near the end of the city limits. Tracey says that despite its square concrete walls, it has the most authentic Mexican food north of L.A. Waiting outside the ugly structure is Eduardo. At least I assume it is he, for when Tracey gets out of the car, the man picks her up in his arms and dances her around the parking lot. Then he carries her back to the car.

"Eduardo, this is Sandi."

I stick out my hand, "Hello. I've heard a lot about you."

"Hi," he says, and then says something to Tracey in Spanish.

Tracey laughs.

"What did he say?"

"He said you would be as pretty as I am if you would smile more."

I am stung by his rudeness. And when we all pile back into the car, I look for reasons not to like him.

His complexion is dark as spice, with straight black hair the color and texture of a horse's mane. His eyes match the color of his skin, with a healthy ring of white surrounding the pupils. Like Tracey, he is fleshy but not fat, a man of strength rather than laziness. I stare at his mouth and chin, both of which are smeared with a shiny coat of Vaseline.

He catches me staring at him.

"Dishwashing," he says. "Chapped lips."

I look away. Tracey is right. There is something very compelling about this man, some deep sort of intelligence.

"Here we are," Tracey says.

"Here we are where?" I ask. "I thought we were driving Eduardo home."

"We are, silly. But we thought we'd have a drink first."

"It's after midnight."

"So?"

"I still have a headache," I say.

"We'll go home soon, I promise."

We go into the pub. It is a Thursday night; the bar is fairly empty. We grab a booth in the back. Tracey lights up a French cigarette. Eduardo and Tracey order two Mexican beers. I have a soda.

"So, you are writer?" Eduardo says to me in English. The words come stintingly but are not heavily accented.

"Yes," I say.

"You write criticism of government?"

"No. Well, I could, but I don't. I write short stories."

"Short stories?" he says, unsure of the term.

"Stories. Fiction?" I look at Tracey for help.

She translates.

His eyes light up in comprehension.

"Sí. How come no criticize government?"

"I just feel there are people better qualified than myself."

"Here in United States, we all qualified," Eduardo says. "I wash dishes, but I qualified. Jack owns restaurant, he qualified. Even beautiful Tracey qualified. This is what I learn in United States. That we can all criticize."

"But Argentina isn't a dictatorship anymore," I say.

"No," he says. "But many many poor people. Like homeless here. Poor people have no say."

He picks up his empty beer glass. "Beautiful Tracey, we have more beer?"

"I'll get it," I say, and stand up to go to the bar.

When I return, Tracey and Eduardo are speaking Spanish very rapidly. I feel lost, foreign, and despite his earlier rudeness, I experience a wave of compassion for Eduardo being so far away from home.

I hand them the beers.

"Thanks, Snatty," Tracey says.

She and Eduardo hold hands and resume their conversation. Every few moments, Tracey looks at me as though expecting me to join in.

Suddenly, Tracey and Eduardo stand up. "Time to go," Tracey says.

"I go to washroom," Eduardo say. "You wait."

We wait.

"That was fun, wasn't it?" Tracey asks.

"I would have preferred if you spoke English, so I could follow," I say. I hear my mother's voice echoing in my head, telling me that this is not the sort of statement that a good guest should make. Almost since my arrival in Santa Cruz, I have felt out of sorts, as though there's a heavy rock in my belly, pulling me down.

"Tomorrow," Tracey says. "Tomorrow we all will speak English. Because we are going to have a party in your honor." And then she hugs me.

The next morning, I wake up early, the sun streaming in through the window of Tracey's guest bedroom. I dress quickly, in jeans and a short-sleeved cotton sweater. Going upstairs to the kitchen to make some tea, I find Tracey already out on the patio, reading a paper.

We decide to go out for breakfast at some muffin and juice shop that Tracey knows. Then we go shopping at the supermarket to buy food for the party.

We buy tons of food: fresh crab salad, three types of cheeses, four types of crackers, blue-green broccoli, sunny lemons, a long loaf of sourdough bread, and blood red raspberries. By the time we get back from the supermarket, it does look like a celebration. Tracey has bought streamers and a half-dozen incense candles that she's strewn all over the living room, as well as six bottles of André pink champagne. The food packages litter the kitchen countertops.

"I thought I'd make a raspberry torte for dessert," Tracey says.

"I didn't know you knew how to make torte."

"I've got a cookbook. How hard could it be? We've got all day, don't we? In fact, why don't we have some champagne now, just to get started?"

Tracey expertly pops the cork of the first champagne bottle. She pours a glass for herself and then one for me.

"You know I don't drink, Tracey," I say.

"Don't give me that. I've seen you drunk, remember?"

"My one and only time. And that was because you insisted that I couldn't graduate from college without once getting drunk in my life."

Tracey laughs. I laugh, too, remembering how the week before I graduated, I had gotten just drunk enough to summon the courage to pick a bunch of wildflowers from the back of the college arboretum and deliver the bouquet to the college president's house with a note begging her to fail me so I wouldn't have to leave Mount Holyoke.

I remember also how on the morning after, Tracey came softly into my room with a glass of fresh-squeezed orange juice and two aspirin in case I felt hung over.

Recalling this, the strange hardness, the tight ball that has been inside my belly since I arrived, vanishes.

Now, Tracey pours orange juice in my champagne to dilute the taste. "Mimosas," she says.

I take one gaily. It takes me all afternoon to drink it. Tracey offers to fix me a new drink while we dress for dinner. I am about to refuse, when we hear a car door slam.

"Damn," Tracey says. "They're early."

"They?"

"Eduardo and Alfredo."

"Alfredo?"

"He's a friend of Eduardo's," Tracey says. "Eduardo thought you would be good together. A surprise for you."

I feel my belly tighten up.

"Tracey, you should have asked me first. I don't want a date."

"It's not a date. He'll just round out the party, that's all."

"But..."

"Oh, Sandi, lighten up. Can't you just relax for one evening? God, you make me crazy sometimes."

"I make myself crazy, too," I say, but already she has turned away.

The next few hours feel like a blur to me, perhaps because Tracey has turned down all the lights, throwing the dark room into shadows cast by a few incense candles that flicker and waver as they burn.

Eduardo, Alfredo, and Tracey finish the remaining bottles of champagne with dinner, switch to white wine and finally to beer.

At some point, I am dancing with Alfredo to Latin dance music, despite the fact that he has yet to utter a single word.

Silently, he and I dance. The sickening sweet smell of burning incense irritates my contact lenses. Alfredo presses his body closer. I can scarcely breathe. I pull away and run out onto the balcony for some air. I breathe the fresh air in deep, trying to catch my breath, to clear my mind of the haze of incense and cigarettes.

I hear Tracey laughing hysterically in the living room. Then I feel him touch my arm.

It is Eduardo. He has followed me out onto the balcony.

"So," he says. "You not like Alfredo."

I close my eyes, then open them, trying to moisten my dry contacts. I focus on the stars.

"I just met him," I say.

"He's a good man. My comrade," Eduardo says. "He asks me why you seem so sad. I ask my Tracey the same thing. She said it is just your way. Why is it your way?"

I notice suddenly that his verb tenses have amazingly improved. He obviously understands far more English than he lets on.

"It's just how I am, I guess," I say.

"I think you just need to learn how to relax. I know a trick that will help. Shall we try it?"

"Depends on what it is," I say, suddenly very wary. Even after eating, Eduardo's mouth is still shiny with a coating of Vaseline.

He pulls a red handkerchief out of his pants pocket. "A game of trust."

"Oh, no," I say. "I don't want to."

I look around for Tracey. Tracey is there on the balcony, too, watching me. "It's all right, Sandi," she says. Her voice is shivery as silver. "It's just a game."

I look at Tracey. Ever since I have known her, she has pushed me to take risks, to come out of my shell that protects me from all my fears. To come out of my shell that keeps me from really living life.

From the living room, I hear the stereo playing loudly. "Okay," I say nervously to Eduardo. "Okay, I'll play."

He takes the handkerchief and ties it around my head like a blindfold. I can feel the edges of the cloth pressing against my eyelids. I can't believe how terrifying it feels to be instantly blind. Eduardo grabs my hand, "Follow me. I'll lead you."

"No! I've had enough. Please."

"It is all right, Sandi," Tracey says again. "Alfredo and I are going to have a quick smoke and then we'll come, too."

The smell of incense is strong within my nostrils, and the air grows warmer. Eduardo has led me inside.

"Come along," he says, pulling at my hand.

"Where are we going?"

"Downstairs. Here is the first step. Don't trip."

I feel like I am stepping into nothingness. Each time I put my foot out, I feel nothing but air, no ground beneath me. Just as I feel I am about to fall, my foot hits the step below me. By the time we reach the last one, my body is shaking.

I raise my hands to tear the handkerchief off my head, away from my eyes, but Eduardo pulls my hands away, clasping them in his.

"No," he says. "Not yet."

He pushes me along the hallway, then tells me to sit down.

"Where?" I say.

"Right below you. Just sit down."

I know in a second that I am on a bed.

I try to stand up, to pull away, but his heavy thighs are locked around my legs. His hands are already on me. I can feel him moving his hands up my stomach to my breasts.

I feel tears wet the bandanna that still covers my eyes. I begin to beg, "Please. Please. Please stop."

"Sssh, sssh," he says. "I won't hurt you."

"Please. Please stop."

He does stop. But only for a moment, while he undoes his zipper, his thighs still holding my body and hands in a tight bruising lock. Then he slowly pulls my shaking hands to his penis.

"Touch this," he says. "This is real, all this. Real. Nothing else. Your words. Stories. Nothing. They are nothing. You are nothing! Only this. Only this is real. Isn't it good? Doesn't it feel good?"

I am thinking—no, I could not think. Only a pulse, like a prayer, beats in my head. This is not happening, this is not happening, this is not happening. This is not, could not, be happening to me. Over and over I say it to myself, a magic litany, so as not to feel his hard penis poking out of the metal zipper, so as not to hear those shiny jellied lips telling me I am nothing.

Suddenly I scream. It is not a scream of horror or pain. It just comes out, a scream of oblivion, a conviction deep within me that if I scream loud enough it will all go away.

I scream and scream, my head twisting about on the bed, fighting him. I twist back and forth until the handkerchief falls off, but I dare not open my eyes. Dare not look at the greasy mouth, his body and what his hands are forcing me to do. I just keep screaming.

And it works. For I feel his hands let go of mine, feel the weight of his thighs leave my legs. I feel the room go lighter.

And suddenly, finally, she is there. Tracey is there, holding me in her arms.

"Sandi, it's me. It's okay. It's me."

Tracey rocks me gently back and forth in her arms, until my screams turn to sobs and my sobs to quiet tears. Then I hear the sound of heavy footsteps.

He is coming back! And he has Alfredo with him. I clutch tighter to Tracey's waist, too frightened to move. The footsteps stop. I hear the front door slam. The men are gone.

I fall into a dark, exhausted sleep.

The next morning I awake at five, call a taxi to come pick me up, and go to the airport. I leave without saying goodbye.

The story is over. I look at Dr. Lane. Our eyes meet. When I had told my sister Linda what had happened a few months earlier, I had not been as graphic as I have just been with Dr. Lane. Though my hands shake from sharing such a secret, Dr. Lane is the first to look away.

"So how do you feel now about the incident?" she asks.

"Confused. Scared. Wondering if I could have done something differently."

"What would you have done?"

"I should have left the minute I met him. I should have listened to what my stomach was telling me."

"So why did you stay?"

"Because I felt guilty for not liking him. Because he was Tracey's boyfriend and loyalty dictated that I try to like him for her sake. That's the hardest thing."

"What is?" Dr. Lane says.

"He frightened me. He could have hurt me. But much, much worse is how Tracey betrayed me. I loved her. I trusted her. She must have known what he was going to do. She should have stopped him."

"Well, maybe she was afraid of him, too," Dr. Lane says.

I feel Dr. Lane is asking me to have compassion. I want to. A few weeks ago I told Tracey that I forgave her. But I know I really haven't. I want to be able to forgive Tracey. And my mother. And Daria. And all the people I have loved who have hurt me.

But I think if I forgive them, I will stop being angry. And if I stop being angry, I will fall apart.

I cannot afford to fall apart.

FEBRUARY 16

Wrote ten more pages of "Graduation Ball," a story that raises the issues of blackness and whiteness in America, a result of all the thinking I've been doing about racism. All that is needed now is the ending and a lot of tightening up. The transitions are nothing. I can't make them all hang together.

Perhaps the problem stems from writing the story in the first person. It feels awkward to me—the writer and the character's persona interfere too much. Yet despite my use of the first person, the story feels distant, far away.

Carrie Lerner, the protagonist, seems to be aping emotions, not feeling them.

All quarter—ten weeks' work—to come up with twenty-two pages of nothing?

I am dreadfully angry with myself.

My esteem for Anna Rothstein, my writing professor, has risen tenfold. It has been increasing steadily in the past few weeks, as she has become more organized in class, and more human to me.

I thought her graceless, awkward in manner and appearance; perhaps she is all that, but she is also honest, and has the courage to say when she is wrong, and the courage to call for peace between men and women.

And I've been so troubled by my Gender and Mass Culture class lately, troubled by what I have been reading, even more troubled by the almost fanatical deification of the Feminist that I see rampant among some of the students.

And troubled by writing this paper on pornography, trying to understand Nathan's obsession with it, and my pain and confusion concerning Santa Cruz.

Everything I read only troubles me more. The Marxist critique falls flat because it argues that men "need" pornography to make up for their powerless state in the capitalist system. But in that case, women, who are even more "powerless" in such a system, would need to read pornography, too. Of course, some do, but not to the same extent as men.

Then there is the mass-culturalist view that romance novels are women's pornography, that women read them because they are titillated by the implied violence of the "heroes," and that women secretly wish to be raped. This view makes me feel sick inside, knowing it's a lie. (Though I applaud critic Janice Radway from the University of Pennsylvania, who argues that romance novels sell not because women wish to be physically and emotionally dominated by the male protagonist, but because during most of the novel the heroine matches wits with the hero, sparring with him verbally and sexually; and though in the end the woman inevitably falls into the standard wifely role, she also has somewhat "tamed" the hero.)

Then there is the militant feminist view, to which I initially thought I would be sympathetic. Emotionally, I do want to be sympathetic, their cries are so compelling, offer such an easy answer. But their answer, to ban all pornography, will not necessarily stop the prevailing societal attitudes and may result in censorship.

Into all of this confusion comes Anna Rothstein's latest book, in which she has the courage, as a woman, as a lesbian known for her strong feminist stance, to deplore some of the feminists' more rabid attacks against pornography.

As for myself, all I know is that I fear Ideology at any level, that while I long for an equal society, a place where I no longer have to walk the streets afraid, or defend who I am, ideology itself can prove to be equally dangerous. For ideology can ultimately lead to fanaticism, at which point Reason is completely destroyed.

This may sound strange coming from me, someone for whom emotions, not rationality, provide the foundation. But my emotions are mine, individual, and belong solely to me, and in the world of Ideology there will be no individualism left. This is what Anna has had the courage to say, and now gives me the strength to say as well.

FEBRUARY 28

Progressing slowly but surely on my essay on pornography. I worked at a feverish pitch yesterday, but today the impetus has left me.

Had tea with Marianne Smithson. It turns out that she has already published a poem in *The Seattle Review.* I am devastated by this news, not to mention in awe of her. Younger than me, she is already published.

I am fiercely jealous.

FEBRUARY 29 (Leap Year)

The faculty dance concert goes up Friday. I haven't really written much about the rehearsals for it, or working with the choreographer Karol. I will never have that sleek, unified look I crave. I do not believe that I will be bad in this performance; merely that I will go unnoticed. All emphasis will be on Daria's piece, anyway, which is the final one in the concert.

But today in ballet class a wonderful thing happened. We were doing the *grand allegro,* a sixteen-count combination that ended with a giant *glissade assemble.* We had done the combination through about one and a half times, in groups of two, trying to utilize all the space in the room, when suddenly Daria signaled Gregory to stop playing.

We students fell silent, knowing that she was about to correct someone. And since she was actually stopping the class to make the correction, we all knew that it would be a big one. I felt myself withdraw, knowing that the directions would likely be for Katherine or Marcela, since these two dancers are the main stars of Daria's piece and she has been riding them hard these past few weeks in preparation for the concert.

But for the first time in months, Daria's attention was turned on me. "Sandi," she said, her voice summoning me to stand in front of the room.

I walked to the front of center stage, pulling down the back of my leotard so that no one standing behind me got the full view of my fleshy butt.

"Sandi has these killer eyes," Daria told the class. "She has these killer eyes and these long silky lashes that take up nearly her entire face. For six years I've been staring at these lashes. And today it just dawned on me that that's why you don't register onstage."

"What?" I said.

"I want you to run back to the corner and take the whole combination from the beginning and make sure that you dance with your eyes open."

Obediently, I started to head towards the corner, but then turned back to look at her, confused.

"I don't understand, Daria. I always dance with my eyes open."

"No, you don't. I just realized that. You look down when you dance, so all we see are the lashes. I want you to do the combination and look directly at my raised hand the whole time."

To demonstrate, she raised her right hand high above head.

I ran back to the corner, my stomach beginning to tingle with excitement. Could this be all that has kept me back all these years?

Gregory gave me a four-count piano introduction. I began the combination.

"Eyes," Daria yelled at me every time I jumped. "Eyes, eyes, eyes."

I stared at her raised hand. I opened my eyes as wide as they would go, straining the lower and upper muscles of my eyelids to keep my eyes round and open. I dared not even blink.

"Yes, yes, yes," Daria said when I made it across the room. "You do it just like that in Karol's piece next week and you'll bring the house down."

My heart soared with pride and joy. I also felt a terrible tightness in my chest, a tight rage that it had taken Daria six years to gift me with this important information.

I waited for her to say something to me after the final *révérence,* to come up to me after class and tell me that the past has all been a mistake, that from now on so long as I kept my eyes open, I would be her number-one dancer, but as soon as class ended she was already in a huddle with Marcela and Katherine, going over some changes in her piece. She didn't even notice me, when at last, disappointed, I slipped out of the room.

MARCH 4

The dance concert.

It went fairly well; I kept my eyes open and made no serious mistakes. As usual, the performance itself went so quickly that just as I was enjoying being onstage, it was over.

Surprisingly, despite a large audience, I wasn't nervous. I knew I understood Karol's choreography. He seemed pleased by our performance, but as he is a very reticent man it is hard to know what he really thought. And ensemble dancing—well, it's about ensemble, not about me or anyone else. It's how George Balanchine once described ballet; a dancer's only function is to illustrate the music.

Afterwards, there was a big reception in the lobby of Meany Theater. Cocktail glasses clinked, people stood in clumps chattering, jewelry dripped off the necks of well-dressed women, glittering under the large lobby lights.

I walked through the lobby in my jeans, my hair stiff from gel and hairspray, a few traces of pancake makeup still blotching my cheeks. A few audience members glanced at me, saw that I was no one of importance and went back to their conversations, their eyes glazing over like the blind marble statues in the Renaissance wing at the MOMA in New York. In statues, blindness is a thing of beauty, round orbs of pearly blue translucence.

But it was such looks from audience members that made me decide to end my professional dancing career two years ago, and perhaps it is why until last week, when Daria stressed the importance of my directly connecting with the audience, I couldn't truly meet the audience's eye.

My first and last paid role as a dancer was as "The Duck" in the children's ballet *Peter and the Wolf.* The Duck is the comic character in the ballet, the one who foolishly allows herself to get eaten by the wolf. I wore a round, white feathered costume that nearly hid my body and bright orange swim-fins on my feet. The biggest choreographic challenge in the role was finding a way to run around the stage without tripping over my own webbed feet.

After giving twelve years of my life to dancing, to taking daily technique classes, surviving an endless number of bloody toes from breaking in new *pointe* shoes every few weeks, wearing small weights on my feet every night to bed in the hope that doing so would improve the curve of my arch, staring, staring endlessly at that studio mirror hoping that one day the vision I saw in my head actually would be reflected in the glass, I was now being paid to run around a stage in bright orange flippers while an audience of six- and seven-year-olds laughed at my awkward, unsuccessful attempts to get away from the wolf.

And after I have at last been eaten, the wolf killed, and Peter and the pretty Bluebird who helped him on his hunt walk off into the painted backdrop of a sunset, the children would come back- stage to talk with their favorite characters. We did eight perform- ances at four different schools in Western Massachusetts, and not once did a single child come up to talk with me. I didn't blame them; when I was six years old and starstruck by the perfect ballet beings I saw onstage, I would never have talked to a giant duck in orange swim-fins, either.

When I said something about my feelings to the artistic director who ran the very small regional company, she told me that "The Duck" was the prime character role, a chance to use my skills as an actress, perfect for the older dancer. I was only twenty-three years old, but her words told me what my fate would be. The next week, I wrote away for catalogs for graduate creative writing programs across the country.

Now as I near the exit of the Meany Studio lobby, I hear a bright voice sing above the din of the crowd: "Mother, come here, I want you to meet Daria George. I want you to meet her."

I leave before I can watch Daria walk over to the dancer's parents, smile graciously, and say wonderful things about the daughter's feet, talent, abilities, opportunities. Say wonderful things that she never quite managed to say to my own parents; only that I tried hard, that I was smart, that a dancer's life was difficult.

Sometimes I feel that I am only imagining a relationship between Daria and me, the way I once imagined that hard work was the only requirement for success.

I leave the building and look out at the late winter sky. The tall brick monolith that guards the university's two main libraries is my only companion. Silently, the monolith and I listen to the sounds of the cars as they rush down University Way.

March 7

Read Margaret Atwood's first novel, *Surfacing*. Nameless woman looking for herself, trying to make sense of her abortion, her married lover, her dead parents, the modern world. She journeys into the Canadian wetlands, turns into the animal she believes she was born as, an animal unable to hurt, or go to war, or lie, or turn into a machine. She is a woman lost, who goes to extremes to find herself again, for whom language holds no meaning.

And for me…why are words inadequate? I feel mummified in this body of mine. My words echo off the soft innards of my flesh, all dark red and soft and warm inside. Like steel bullets lodged in a person's throat, the thoughts and ideas and feelings ricochet inside my body, but have no place to exit—the words and ideas and thoughts must not, dare not escape through my mouth.

For in the outside world, the ideas will grow cold and solid and mechanical. The life will be gone, no breathing, sighs, half-whispered hopes. Daily I retreat from people more and more. My contact with them now seems only like a method of keeping time, a ritual I have to go through like sleep, so I can get back to the real world that is happening, growing inside me.

March 10

Of course I got a B- (a low mark unheard of in graduate school) on my pornography paper for my Gender and Mass Culture class. My professor, Justine Clark, said it was extremely well-written stylistically, but I didn't "press" the critical text or offer any valid solutions to the problems. I've never been good at ironing anyway, and since when are literature classes supposed to pose solutions to social ills?

Isn't the role of art simply to bring the problems out into the open? Isn't the role of art simply to write, paint, dance about what gets your juices going?

None of those French critics that Clark is so fond of quoting offer any solutions either; they just tell writers what they are doing wrong.

I will never go for a PhD. I will never go for a PhD. I will never go for a PhD.

MARCH 14

It has been raining steadily now for five days and no end is in sight.

As I watch the rain fall, I wonder if it is doing my weeping for me. I have not cried for a very, very long time. Is all my pent-up restlessness, my sadness merely a call for release?

The last time tears fell was that night in Santa Cruz, when I cried at Tracey's betrayal and at that man's attack on my body and soul. Did my heart break so completely that now it is too cold, icy, and afraid to start pumping again the warm blood of life?

I am tired of all the voices in my head, the endless worrying that this time I will not be able to emerge from the depression, that my ups and downs are an early form of insanity. I am tired of attempting to be cheerful over the phone with my parents and friends, as though there is nothing wrong, as though I don't feel myself growing humorless and narrow from self-absorption.

Anna Rothstein once accused one of my characters of being an "old maid," not so much sexually but in spirit. Is this happening to me? Am I going to live my life in half-shadows, like Faulkner's Miss Emily, dreaming of things I cannot have?

Instead, I watch and write down what I see. I have always been a watcher. Perhaps this is why I failed at dancing, because I cannot get inside the movement, truly feel what an *adagio* is, as opposed to what it looks like. I have stopped feeling again, gone numb, and am only going through the motions of living.

Yesterday, I told Dr. Lane that I wanted to be a writer who uses no words.

"Why?" she says.

"Because words come in varying degrees of pain."

"Very clever," Dr. Lane says.

"Yes," I say. "Very clever."

I take a deep breath. I breathe in and out.

SPRING

If the moon could be so cruel, might it not
be equally kind and grant her wish? She made
a wish: "Let me find it—the Good Thing."
And she repeated it several times on the train,
watching the moon disappear behind the clouds.
She relaxed, inviting the incubus, sleep filling
up her stomach and mind, and drifted into a
dream.

—Charles Johnson, *Faith and the Good Thing*

The camellias are starting to bloom; they look extra pink and delicate next to the tall apartment buildings and the ugly freeway. Somehow they seem more beautiful because the flowers are few and far between, more precious—a fragrant gift.

Perhaps their blossoming inspired me to go downtown and explore.

I got off the bus at Stewart Street and then walked down Fourth Avenue. I passed the Seattle Public Library, so I went in and got a library card. It is a small library as city libraries go; all of it could fit in one wing of the Copley branch in Boston. The books are old, dusty, still embalmed in the old-fashioned red or black cloth covers with fading gold-embossed titles.

I wanted so to breathe life into the stacks, excite them with new stories, new ideas, my words. And yet I liked the place; it felt both foreign and familiar, like stumbling across your grandmother's antique linen chest and going through it drawer by drawer.

To keep the feeling going, I decided to journey down to Pioneer Square, the oldest part of the city, the part that, in 1854, went up in flames. Local lore has it that as the saloons and whorehouses (one of which was run by a "Madam Damnable" and also doubled as the county courthouse) burned, thousands of rats came up from the basement of these wooden tenements and poured out into the streets.

Some of the more upstanding citizens of the town, including the Women's Christian Temperance Union, took the fire as a sign from God that Seattle must mend its ways. Soon after, these same women began raising money to build what is now the University of Washington, hoping that the school would have a calming influence on their sons (of course no one thought about the daughters).

One hundred years later, greed having replaced sex as the vice of choice, Pioneer Square now hosts a series of expensive art galleries, the famed Elliott Bay Book Company, jazz clubs, and restaurants, all aimed at Seattle's large tourist trade. It is also a gathering place for most of Seattle's homeless, who, standing underneath a beautifully carved twelve-foot totem pole (the last remnant of a destroyed culture), beg for money from those same tourists.

I myself was drawn to an art gallery on First Avenue which displayed an odd sort of tapestry and cloth collages by an Israeli artist. The gallery curator saw me staring at the collages' bold bright colors and came up to talk. She could tell at once I was without resources, would not be able to purchase a thing, yet she walked me around the whole gallery, asking my opinion of each piece.

I think she just genuinely enjoyed talking with people, and since the shop was empty of customers, I helped her break the monotony of waiting for a sale. It made me feel good to talk with her, and I left the shop smiling.

I walked back down First Avenue and headed for the pier, where I watched the large white ferryboats carry their passengers across Elliott Bay. The vast expanse of water is framed by the stunning backdrop of the snowcapped Olympic Mountains.

I bought a hot dog and ice-cream cone from one of the vendors on the pier before taking in a movie at the Omnidome theater. It was an odd experience watching the IMAX films; at first I felt a little airsick, the images loomed so large, moving toward me from the screen, until I decided that the view I saw onscreen was not much different from the overwhelming scenery I had just witnessed outside.

After eight hours downtown, I felt happy and tired and content. And when I got back to the apartment, there was a letter waiting for me from *Art/Life* magazine. It said that they wanted to publish my story "Haymarket Station." My first piece has been accepted for publication!

What an utterly perfect day.

March 20

So I suppose that I have made my deadline: published before the age of twenty-five. I am pleased, of course, and somewhat stunned. I keep thinking that I should feel differently now that I am about to be a published author, but all I can focus on is how much further I have to go, how I must keep writing and writing to uncover whatever talent and ability is inside me. This is not the time to rest, to celebrate; no, right now I must keep the impetus, the movement going. I am lucky now; success is within reach.

At the same time, my mind soars ahead, thinking about having another story published, yet another. It jumps forward to book deals and movie contracts and Pulitzer Prize acceptance speeches. (Ladies and gentlemen, I am grateful to Columbia University for bestowing this great honor upon me. Words cannot express ...)

I tell myself that it is only a small literary magazine with a readership of five hundred. It is only a small magazine that pays in copies because it cannot afford to pay cash.

Words cannot express ...

March 22

All week, I've been up and down like a yo-yo, thrilled about the publication but fearful that the acceptance was only a fluke, that there will be no more.

Got my grades today for the winter quarter. Anna Rothstein give me a 4.0 for my writing class, but all she wrote on my final story, "Graduation Ball," was "Good Luck."

Nothing else, just good luck. How am I to interpret that? Good luck, you'll need it? Good luck with your endeavors—it is hard to do what you are trying to do? Or simply, good luck, like an employee who has just been dismissed?

I am itching, itching to look at Marianne's and Felicia's stories to see what comments she has written on theirs. Is she always this silent? Can these professors really believe that we have so much confidence that we do not need the praise, or the criticis, of others?

Even if someone were to come up to me and say "I hate your work," at least I could say "Why?" Then he or she would have to talk about the work itself—how it affected them, how it disturbed them or angered them.

I do not want to write just pretty sentences, words strung together in a pleasing manner. I am after emotion, movement, self-recognition, and yes, irony.

MARCH 24

Felicia and John (remember them and that birthday party?) are moving to Australia when Felicia receives her MFA this spring. They are leaving America because they feel they cannot survive in this country.

She is a writer, and he—well, it seems he doesn't do much of anything, so they are immigrating to Australia, where there are more opportunities. (Felicia said they had applied two or three years ago but it's taken this long to get the necessary green cards.) The whole situation is pathetic: that Americans must go elsewhere in order to have a better kind of life.

I don't know whether Felicia will make it as a writer in Sydney, though she says they were accepted because there is a shortage of writers and editors there. Still, I can understand her wanting to try somewhere else. I myself keep waiting for the day I go to Europe, though I wonder if I could actually live in Italy for more than a year or two. I wonder if I would be homesick. After all, I buy into the American myth of success as much as anyone. But women or men less ambitious than myself, who are less willing or capable of clawing their way to the top, is there to be no place for them any-more in this country?

Is the United States destined to become a feudal society, with the Lords of Finance and Aggression ruling over the Underclass with great stonewalls separating one from the other?

First day of spring quarter, and already I blew it.

In my novel-writing class taught by Cecil Harris, Harris went around the room asking us what we currently are reading, our influences. I told him that I was currently under the spell of Anais Nin and Milan Kundera.

"Kundera's good," Harris said. "But Nin? That diary."

"What about it?" I said. "It's wonderful. I feel like I'm entering a new world when I read it. Not Paris so much, but her psyche."

"Too self-absorbed," Harris said. And the class nodded sagaciously in agreement.

"So you've read it?"

"That diary," Harris said again.

I sat back in my chair, and though I pretended to listen to his introductory speech about first novels and opening chapters, I was furious. I thought of comeback lines that, if my life were truly a novel and I a daring heroine, I might have said (to put Harris in his place): "Too self-absorbed? John Updike has been writing the same story about his adultery and Protestant guilt over and over again for the last twenty years and they call him a genius. Philip Roth shared his psychoanalysis (and his endless sex fantasies) with the whole world in *Portnoy* and the critics called it a masterpiece. Yet when Nin or any woman dares write about what she feels, how she views the world personally, it's labeled confessional or self-centered or self-absorbed."

I mean, Harris has just published a novel about a unicorn living in a mythological forest—yes, I know it's supposed to be a fable, but a grown man writing about unicorns? It makes me think of those pink unicorns on TV that they market to young girls—I think they are called "Pretty Brite" or something.

And then an hour later in Eve Porter's Literary Genres class, she kept talking about the "usefulness" of fiction, its moral intent, of its power to change the world, etc., almost as though she had been listening in on my rampant thoughts in Harris's class.

Yes, my work is personal. I write so that I may better understand myself and my relationship with the external world that frightens me so. Fiction is the only way I can find the words to the silence that is myself. I cannot do it in my real life, for I, as a physical entity, am coarse. Like in this journal, words in my outside world are used wrongly; only in fiction can I trim the edges, break through the artifice of myself, and find the true human being beneath.

I've never been one to change the world. If I tilt at windmills, they are personal windmills. My dragons are loneliness, fierce ambition, fear, and a mood that changes every hour, every second.

So what if that is being self-absorbed? All writers are. They *must* be to complete the work. They *must* be because the world doesn't really want or need books about unicorns or Protestant adultery or diaries until we writers create that need for them.

MARCH 28

Talking with Dr. Lane about weight and lightness. About floating through life. It is strange because my first novel that I wrote in college was about puppetry, about how the character Paul pulled Julie's strings and how life pulled Paul's. But I suddenly feel as though I am completely stringless, a free agent standing alone with no past. I have no feet, only skim the surface of the physical world while my internal world daily increases in substance.

Daily, I have less and less connection with my body as mine, as belonging to me, as opposed to it being just any body that is made up of flesh and bone and muscle.

How strange for a dancer to be talking like this. But perhaps this distancing from my own body is why I failed. Back then I was terribly aware of my body, of its limitations, how it looked in the mirror; but I felt no connection to it, only the various aches and pains of strained muscles. Now I feel even lighter and am afraid of dematerializing altogether.

Dr. Lane thinks such distancing may have something to do with Santa Cruz, that I am pulling away from my body to protect it from harm.

But I want so to come back to earth, to be grounded, to walk once more among the people of the world and not stay in this strange, floating place.

MARCH 29

Three quarters into my degree and only now they begin indoctrinating me about their rules and regulations. Eve Porter incensed me today by stating that writing is more political (i.e., has more power) than the other arts and therefore has more direct uses for humanity.

Art is Art! Daria's ballet piece about nuclear war is as powerful as anything I've seen written. And she drew her inspiration from a film she had seen.

How supercilious such an attitude is. And even more troubling is Eve's and Cecil Harris's belief that writing must be for the conscious betterment of humanity, that writing must be political to be deemed "worthy." (Oscar Wilde must be laughing himself silly!)

It hurts me to believe that my work is "invalid" because it is not about saving trees or whales or the starving in Africa. What about the starvation of the human heart?

So what am I going to do?

I am going to do a ballet about Santa Cruz. I have decided to do so to prove Eve Porter wrong.

I have decided to do a ballet about Santa Cruz to reclaim my body.

I have decided to do a ballet about Santa Cruz because that is the only way I know how to write about the silent character "Beauty," whom I first envisioned during my first month in Seattle.

I have decided to do a ballet about Santa Cruz because it is spring quarter and I said that in the spring I would attempt a live work.

I have decided to do a ballet about Santa Cruz because I want Daria to finally see that I am capable of handling a dramatic piece onstage.

I have decided to do a ballet about Santa Cruz because I can.

MARCH 30

I talk to Daria about doing my ballet. She says that I can perform it at the student dance concert this June. But I have to attend a regular weekly meeting with the other choreographers to discuss lights and costumes and program order and any other issues that come up in the course of putting a performance together.

I also must get an advisor to supervise the project, in case I run into trouble.

"I thought you would advise me," I say. "A chance for us to finally work together."

"I can't. I already am responsible for two other projects, plus serving as artistic director. With teaching and running the department, there just isn't enough time."

I feel my heart fall to my knees. She is rejecting me once more.

"But you know me," I say. "I can't just ask anyone."

"Ask Karol," Daria says. "You were in his piece last quarter. He likes you."

I am about to call the whole thing off. I am about to say that I don't have time, either. But then I think of myself dancing in *pointe* shoes on the stage. I imagine that I am thin and beautiful and perfect. Daria stares at me, stunned, wondering how she could have been so foolish not to have seen my talent sooner.

"Fine," I say. "Karol will do just fine."

MARCH 31

Kevin, a guy from the Distance Learning office where I work part-time as a copyeditor, has set me up with a friend of his named Sam

Murdoch. Kevin has been trying to get us to go out together for months, but the thought of a blind date terrifies me.

"What's he like?" I ask Kevin.

"Well, he is out of work right now, but starting his own business. And his father has just died, so he's kind of lonely."

"Sounds terrific," I say sarcastically. "Besides, discussion about business bores me."

"Not this business," Kevin says. "He makes movies."

"Oh," I say.

We have had this same conversation for months now, before Brad Baldwin, before Santa Cruz ever happened, but the other day there was a message on my answering machine from this Sam Murdoch. He has the sexiest voice I have ever heard.

So I capitulated. Tonight I agreed to go out with him, providing Kevin came with us and took me home.

"You understand that this is not a date," I say to Kevin for the hundredth time at work.

"I understand."

"I mean, it's only a look. We go to a bar for a few minutes, we talk and then you drive me home. If I like him, then we can talk about a date some other time, okay?"

"Okay," Kevin says. "It will be fine."

So yesterday I went out and bought a brand-new white cotton shirt that looks like linen and makes my skin look tan even in this pale Seattle sun. I will wear it with my olive green pants, so that my hazel eyes will be flecked with emerald under the lights of a bar.

"I hate bars," I tell my suitemate Tanya as I dress for the date. "I don't drink and it's really smoky."

"So why are you going?" the ever-practical Tanya asks. Tanya is a nurse, pursuing her master's in pain management. I like the idea of living with someone who can learn to master pain. It makes me hopeful. It makes me hopeful that if this night is a disaster I can come home and collapse and she can put me back together again.

Kevin picks me up exactly on time. "You look great," he says.

"Let's not do this," I say, as we get into Kevin's car.

"We have to. He's waiting for us at the bar. Look, he's my best friend. I've known him since high school. We did *West Side Story* together."

"Sharks or Jets?" I ask.

"Sharks."

We drive for a few minutes in silence.

"So what does he look like?" I ask casually, as though I don't really care.

"A lot like me. People used to take us for brothers."

Kevin is dark and tall and Spanish-looking and smells like Pierre Cardin aftershave.

We pull into the parking lot of the bar/restaurant, which is located across the street from where we work. It is called The Deluxe II. Until tonight, I never even knew it was there. I think it is a very stupid name for a restaurant.

"I can't do this," I say to Kevin suddenly, filled with panic.

"You know if I wasn't married," Kevin says, "I'd go after you myself. You're smart, pretty."

"Is this a pep talk or are you making a pass?" I say. "Because if you're making a pass I just can't handle this right now."

Kevin laughs, "It will be okay."

We go into the bar. It is dark and murky, but free of cigarette smoke, which I am grateful for. We wind through a series of tables until we come to one upstairs by a window. He is sitting there alone having a drink.

He stands up. He doesn't look a thing like Kevin. He looks like Harrison Ford.

When I put out my hand to shake his, he holds it just for a moment and looks into my eyes. "It is very nice to meet you," he says.

I think he means it.

We sit back down and begin to talk. Somewhere after the first hour, Kevin just drifts away, leaving Sam and me alone. I don't even notice when he leaves.

Somewhere after the second hour, Sam tells me about how his father died snorkeling in the blue, blue waters of the Caribbean. His father was eighty years old.

Sam is thirty-three, never been married, though just came off an eight-year relationship. He has won two Emmy Awards, including one for set design.

I am impressed.

He tells me that he uses the awards as bookends.

I am even more impressed.

Somewhere after the third hour, I tell him about Santa Cruz. I don't mean to tell him, but somehow it all slips out. Maybe I am testing him to see if he blames me or now finds me repulsive, untouchable. Or maybe I just want him to know that I am vulnerable.

He seems to understand, because then he tells me a story about when he went to Vancouver with his high school marching band and one of the girls in the group was being harassed by a bunch of sailors.

"We took those sailors out," Sam says. "They didn't even know what hit them."

Is that what I want? For someone to go beat the hell out of that cruel man in Santa Cruz, until he feels as powerless and helpless as I did?

Still, the idea of violence makes me uneasy; it seems an escalation rather than a solution to the problem. Nonetheless, I feel myself begin to breathe again, knowing that Sam and I have crossed this first bridge together.

It is nearly two a.m. and the bar is about to close. Sam offers to drive me home. We walk out to the parking lot together still talking.

Sam drives a big old pickup truck. I stare at it a few minutes trying to take it in. "This is yours?" I ask, wondering why a man who won two Emmys and wants to direct movies drives a pickup truck. In the cities of the East Coast, people don't drive pickup trucks. They drive small compact cars or BMWs, or take the subway, or maybe—if they are like Nathan Katz—they have a limousine service escort them anonymously (and anyone else they want to hide) to wherever it is anonymous people want to go. But they don't drive mustard-colored pickup trucks.

Question: "Why are they called pickup trucks?"
Answer: "Because they pick up useful things."

I wonder if I have just been picked up. I wonder if he finds me useful.

I stare at the truck some more.

"What's wrong?" he asks.

"I've never been in one of these before," I said. "It's so big."

He laughs.

"I haul around camera equipment," he says. "Heavy lights and smoke machines, etc. Now that I'm freelance, I need to bring a lot of my own stuff. Besides, I'm six-three. I need something I can fit in."

"It's fine," I say, hoping I haven't offended him.

"Get in," he says.

I hop into the cab and strap myself into the passenger seat. He sits on the driver's side. There are about four feet between us.

"You can move closer," he says, and pats the spot next to him.

I undo my seatbelt and slide a little closer along the seat. (It's not really a seat, it's more like a soft bench.)

He does my seatbelt up for me and suddenly we are sitting side by side.

"Where do you live?" he asks.

"On Brooklyn Ave. Stevens Court. It's graduate housing."

As we drive back, we talk about my writing.

"I would really like to see some of your work," he says. "I'm very impressed by writers."

Suddenly, I forget that he is sitting so close to me that I can feel his leg pressing against my thigh. Suddenly I forget that I barely know him. I talk about my work. I talk about wanting to be a writer who uses no words, because words, like blows, come in varying degrees of pain.

He listens quietly. And then we are at my place. He walks me to the door.

"It truly was great to meet you," he says. "Would you like to do it again some time?"

I note that he doesn't give me an exact date. It is up to me. I like that. I also realize suddenly that I want to give him something. To give him some of my work to take home with him.

"Did you really mean what you said about seeing my work?" I ask.

"Of course."

"If you've got a second, then, come on in and I'll give you one of my stories."

We walk in quietly so not to wake my suitemates. With him there, my room feels very, very small. He looks at my computer and printer, while I go through my files trying to find the exact story I want to give him.

I hand him "Graduation Ball."

Then suddenly we are kissing, kissing slowly, kissing passionately, kissing each other's mouths, and ears and foreheads and necks.

We kiss nonstop for about two hours. We kiss until our lips are numb.

Afterwards, we stare at each other dazedly. He invites me to go away with him for the weekend to his family's cabin at a place called Whidbey Island.

Because he has kissed me silly but made no attempts to go further, I trust him.

"Of course I'll go," I say.

We smile.

I walk him to the door.

"I'll call you tonight," he says.

"Okay," I say.

And then he is gone.

It is four in the morning. I get undressed and crawl into bed. I fall asleep at once and do not dream. Who needs to dream?

APRIL 1

I am flying. I am soaring like a bird. I look down at the rest of the world and it seems a distant blur, foreign, awkward, having nothing to do with me who can fly so high.

I feel it in my blood, like a volcano about to explode. Not him so much, but *it*, an excited longing so deeply pleasurable it almost hurts. It boils within me, hot churning liquid that flip-flops in my stomach and does loop-de-loops.

In my Literary Genres class, I have no idea what anyone says. I watch their lips move and wonder why people have such a penchant for talking. I watch their mouths move and smile back. Eve Porter asks me what I think. I smile. I try to make myself stop, to listen seriously to the conversation, but it's like my muscles belong to someone else. Inevitably, my lips slide back, revealing a set of perfectly white, straight teeth courtesy of the orthodontist my parents paid so well when I was twelve to make sure that their sensitive, somewhat dreamy-eyed daughter would have a beautiful smile.

I decide to write my parents a letter and thank them for my teeth.

I decide not to write my parents a letter.

Later at work, I am totally useless. I am supposed to be pasting up a revised version of one of our astronomy study guides. I have already typed up the new changes. Now I just have to cut them down to size and paste them down over the old pages. It is a simple task but requires careful attention. I am not paying attention. I keep having to do the same section over and over again because I forget what I am doing and cut out the wrong words.

"What's wrong with you today?" my boss chides me.

"Nothing," I say and I smile.

From behind his workstation, Kevin laughs at me. I glare at him.

"What?" he says.

"Don't think just because you played Cupid, that makes you special or anything," I say.

"Yeah, right," Kevin says, and laughs again.

I laugh with him.

I call Rachel in Boston. I tell her everything from the beginning, even about Sam's pickup truck.

Rachel grew up in an old mill town in New Hampshire and spent most of her high school years riding around with boys in pickup trucks. She is amused that the concept so blows me away.

"Anyway, he asked me to go away with him this weekend. Some cabin his family has."

"Will his family be there?" she asks.

"I don't know," I say. "I don't think so."

"How are you going to get there?"

"He'll drive me, of course."

"But do you know where this place is?"

"Somewhere on the water, I guess. It's an island."

"Like how far?"

"I don't know."

"Is he seeing someone else?"

"He just broke up with someone. A long relationship."

"Are you his transitional person?"

"I don't know."

"You spend six hours with this guy and now you are going to go away with him?"

"I already said yes," I said.

"So what are you calling me for?"

"I want to know what you think."

"I think maybe you should wait. Why can't you just go out a couple more times on your own turf? Then in a few weeks you can go away."

"But he says he has to go," I say. "If I don't go with him, I won't see him again until Monday."

"You're going to go, aren't you?" Rachel says.

"Of course I am."

She laughs.

"Have a really good time," she says. "Call me when you get back."

"Of course," I say, and hang up the phone.

As soon as I put the receiver down, it rings again.

"Hello, hello?" I say.

It is Sam. My heart pounds.

"I just wanted to call to make sure you were real," he says. "I wanted to make sure I wasn't dreaming all this."

"It's real," I say.

"Oh God," he says.

"Exactly," I say.

He hangs up.

Friday is twelve hours away.

APRIL 2

He arrives at my door with flowers. Nothing too big, just two red roses intermixed with baby's breath. We stare at each other a moment, making sure that we are in person who we remember each other to be.

He wears blue jeans, a flannel work shirt and a red rain slicker from REI. He looks the very essence of the Pacific Northwest.

"Come on in," I say. "You can meet my suitemates."

"The truck's double-parked," he says. "We can only stay a minute."

"I'm ready," I say. "Let me just go get my stuff."

My suitemates are in the living room, conveniently finishing up dinner. I hear them laughing and talking politely to Sam while I run to my room to get my weekend suitcase. His voice is very deep and male and rises up over the voices of the others. I like the sound of it.

I contemplate whether I should take my ski jacket, which is black and white and makes me look like a stuffed penguin. I have yet to wear it since I've been out here, but over the phone Sam had told me to pack warm clothes. I decide to leave it behind and, instead, throw another sweater into my suitcase. I grab my raincoat and join them in the living room.

"I'm ready," I say.

"Great," he says.

Then to my suitemates, he says, "It was very nice to meet you."

"Well, have a good time," Alda says.

"Be careful," Pieta says.

"Be yourself," Tanya says.

Their advice is just an echoing of the voices in my head which, as I follow Sam out to the truck, are telling me the very same things.

As we head north to the interstate, we talk casually about our respective days. He tells me stories about working as a freelancer— the people he has met. Back when he worked at KIRO television (Seattle's CBS affiliate), he spent the day with Dan Rather.

"I was the floor director," Sam says. "It was my job to make talent feel comfortable. To make sure they had the clothes they need, something to drink, knew where their marks were onstage. Anyway, Dan was a really nice guy. All the office bigwigs were afraid of him, kowtowing to him, calling him "Mr. Rather" and rushing around like crazy whenever he was around. I took him to the Space Needle for lunch. We talked about Seattle and his family and lots of different things. He was just like everyone else. That's what I learned in TV, that famous people are just like us."

"Did you meet a lot of writers?" I ask.

"Sure," he says. "They came through on tour promoting their books."

"Like who?" I say.

He laughs, "I don't remember their names. Like I said, after eight years in television, everyone seems like your average guy."

I think suddenly of Nathan Katz, writing his television scripts while high on cocaine and watching porno flicks.

I think of the ballet dancers I knew in New York, the day that Leslie Browne (who starred in the film The Turning Point) took a class at my studio. She stood right behind me at the barre. She looked much smaller in person. She did the exact same exercises I did. She just did them much, much better. If a whisper hadn't gone through the room announcing her arrival at the start of class, I never even would have known she was there. She was just one more talented dancer taking class, working hard to perfect her craft.

"Maybe because famous people are always depicted as bigger and better than life, so we don't recognize them when we see them on the street," I say. "It's their way of keeping the world away."

After that we compare our lists of our ten all-time favorite movies. We sing songs from West Side Story. Then suddenly in the darkness, Sam pulls the truck to a halt.

"What's wrong?" I say.

"Ferry traffic," he says. "Looks like a long wait."

"We're taking a ferry?"

"Sure," he says. "I thought I told you. The Mukilteo ferry."

I panic, trying to recall in the blur that has been the past seventy-two hours since I met him all that he has told me.

"Yeah," I say. "I guess you did."

Are there other things he has said that I've forgotten?

We stare at each other in darkness, the truck parked in the darkness waiting for the arrival of the next boat. We have run out of conversation, so we turn to each other and kiss in the darkness.

There are cars surrounding us on all sides, but Sam simply draws me to him and we kiss.

I feel the tension melt out of me.

Forty-five minutes later as we drive onto the ferry, I sit in the crook of his arm, sipping a cup of hot chocolate that he bought me from the coffeeshop at the ferry terminal. With a noisy whoosh, the boat departs from the dock. We leave the land behind. I look back to see the lights from the Mukilteo houses twinkle and dance.

In front of us, there is only water and a starless sky.

APRIL 3

By the time we arrive at the cabin, it has begun to rain. A real rain, which falls upon our heads with a weighty, consistent rhythm as we unpack the truck.

The wind rustles the tall trees with a throaty sigh. I tilt my head up to watch the branches and leaves dance, forming odd patterns against the nighttime sky. A single dog barks at the wind. I cringe, reach for Sam's hand.

He's not there.

I fumble for the flashlight that he had given me when we drove up. The beam is weak, pale, and I peer out between the raindrops, searching. He is on the ground by the side of the cabin digging in the dirt.

"What are you doing?" I ask.

"Turning on the water," he says. "We turn it off in the winter so the pipes don't burst. We cover the plumbing with the dirt because it keeps the pipes from freezing."

"Oh," I say.

Do my parents cover their pipes in the winter? In New York, it snows much more often than here, yet I never recall my father sneaking out to cover his spigots or sprinklers. Maybe he did it at night when I slept.

I put my hand on the rough stone wall of the cabin to make sure it is real.

At last, Sam digs the key out of his pocket and unlocks the door and switches on the lights. It is freezing inside; the island dampness has settled into the wood-paneled walls. But there is a giant picture window running along one whole side of the cabin and revealing a beautiful view of the Sound.

And there is a large brick fireplace that sits in the center of the room.

"I'll have it warm in a jiffy," Sam says, and goes outside to fetch wood from a huge cord piled behind the house.

I shiver helplessly and look around for something to do. An antique silver teakettle sits on the top of the old Hotpoint stove. I let the water run in the sink for a moment, listening to the gurgle of the pipes as they start up again. Then I begin filling the kettle for tea.

"Don't do that!" Sam says, returning with an armload of wood.

"You don't like tea?"

"Don't use that water. It's bitter, not treated. You could get sick."

"But it's coming out of the sink. It's not rusty or anything."

"It's not for drinking," he says. "We use it for washing up, doing dishes. You just can't drink it. That's why we bought all that bottled water at the store. I thought you'd know."

"I didn't," I say, miserably.

Everything about this place is strange and alien, even him.

"It's okay," he says, and rubs my cheek with his left hand.

He has large rough hands, with long, thick fingers swollen from the physical labor of tearing down and putting up hundreds of heavy, metal Hollywood lights and gels. From putting up wooden scaffolding that on film is transformed into a castle wall or the side of a barn.

"The director has the vision," Sam had told me a few minutes ago. "The cinematographer has the eye. But the grip, the grip is the one who actually builds the illusion."

I believe him to be a great illusion-maker, for despite the coarseness of his skin, when he touches me I feel like I am being stroked by warm silk.

Our desire hangs between us like a taut electrical wire.

When the fire burns hot and strong—blue-yellow flames hungrily lapping up paper, wood, anything it finds—we unfold the worn, green Castro convertible until the head of the bed is just a few feet from the flames, and we undress.

Before we press our bodies together, Sam holds up a small box of condoms. "Do we need these?" he asks.

I have already inserted my diaphragm when I washed up in the tiny bathroom, but I know that birth control is not what he is asking about.

"You were with, Carol, wasn't it, how long?" I ask.

"Eight years."

I draw in a breath. "Were you ever unfaithful?"

"Once," he says, without hesitating. "Near the end of the relationship."

I want to trust him. I want to show him that I trust him.

I wait for him to ask about me. Including him, I will have been with four men in the past seven years. I have never considered myself promiscuous, but suddenly I begin to wonder if people ever view themselves that way.

"I think we'll be okay," I say.

He grins and puts the box back into his suitcase.

As he puts the condoms away, I feel a strange flutter in my stomach. I know in my head that we should use them. I know exactly why AIDS is spreading like wildfire throughout this country.

I know that when he takes me into his arms and kisses me, I won't think about it again until after we are done. Then I will think about my decision with regret and worry about it for weeks afterwards.

I know that I will not tell him that I am worried.

So now we are lovers trying to find our way. The rain ceased during the night and now the sky is a miraculous blue.

We walk the beach, a narrow strip of rocky sand dotted with madrona trees. Only four or five feet separate the land from the water, so often we must climb over large pieces of driftwood to continue our sojourn down the beach.

Small cliffs built of rock and sand and trees hang out over the beach like giant bowsprits of schooners, expertly carved by nature's most famous artists: erosion, wind, and time. The water is gray and murky, and terribly cold. Sam says that in winter or summer, its temperature rarely rises above fifty degrees. I shiver at the notion and think longingly of the vast white silky beaches of my Long Island childhood. Every spring, when the late-May sun began melting the tar on the streets, my friends and I would cut school early and ride our bicycles to Long Beach or Malibu. Hot and sticky from the journey, we would throw ourselves into the bobbing whitecaps of the Atlantic Ocean.

I blush suddenly, recalling that one of my first true sexual moments took place at Malibu. It was nearing dusk and we needed to get home for dinner. The air had cooled as the sun waned, and as we emerged from the water, our bodies drenched, the brisk sea air made my fourteen-year-old nipples pucker and pulsate, a sensation so utterly new and exquisite that it stopped me dead in my tracks.

"Wait," I called out to my friends, who had already begun moving down the beach towards the showers and bike racks.

I stood there for a moment more, waiting for it to happen again, but as my friends turned around to come back for me, the moment was already lost.

Later on, as we wheeled our bicycles back up the street, still thrilled by my discovery, I asked, "Isn't it strange how the wind makes your nipples hard?"

My two girlfriends gave me a quick stare, then raised their eyebrows at each other in exasperation.

My mood vanished at once. I had committed a huge faux pas, though to this day I am not sure whether it was because they thought me too old to be so naive or because "nice" girls kept such secrets to themselves.

Whatever the reason for their silent but obvious disapproval, I carried the memory of that cold stare with me for many years. It was perhaps one reason I waited so long to take my first lover. Even then, even in the midst of my pleasure, a part of me always held back, fearful that I might say or do the wrong thing.

I look over at Sam walking alongside me. He pulls out a harmonica from his jeans pocket and begins to play. He plays well, a familiar sea chanty. He plays without a trace of self-consciousness. He plays without fear of judgment or recrimination. For this I decide that I can fall in love with him.

But I do not tell him my story. Instead I write it down here, recording all my hurts and joys and moments of shame.

APRIL 6

To satisfy my Literary Genres class requirements, Eve Porter has agreed to let me keep a journal about the experience of creating *Ways of Being, 1988*. (This is the title I have decided upon for the piece about my silent character who will dance upon the stage. Her name is no longer "Beauty," but "Janie.") Just the fact that I am consciously recording the experience for someone else to read makes me question its authenticity. I fear that the writing will be too constructed, that my thoughts about the piece will become as "fictive" as the piece itself. Still, as a technician, the idea pleases me: the creation of a creation of a creation of an artist.

Anyway, tonight I wrote and recorded the text. After all these months thinking about the piece, sorting through all the different ideas I want to explore, it seems almost ludicrous to reduce it to a text of only three paragraphs. Eight minutes long with the addition of the music at the end.

Theatrical writing is different from straight fiction. I find myself being less specific, going after whole concepts rather than creating an individual. It is the dancing that will create Janie; dancing is the only way she can speak. I've used clichés for the script, in an attempt to capture the way people talk about other people, the way a gossip talks about a person he or she doesn't really know.

I envision something professional. I fear it will be amateur. My limited audio equipment makes the prose sound silly, not hollow. And ideally, I would like professional actors to record the various parts on tape, not me. (Though Sam did agree to tape the voice-over role of the rapist for me. Strange irony that: one's new lover playing the role of a rapist.)

I need the appropriate balance between violence and understatement for the rape sequence. It is the high point of the dance. Everything is so beautiful in ballet, and here I want to use this most beautiful medium to convey ugliness.

This is a piece about contrasts.

APRIL 8

I join Daria and the five other choreographers for our first meeting at By George, a rather busy café on campus. The meeting is at 7:30 a.m., and I arrive late and sleepy, having stayed up most of the night working on a short story.

We each go around in a circle, introducing ourselves. Many I know from ballet class, though I never actually talked to any of them beyond a perfunctory hello while warming up at the *barre*.

Daria talks about a tight time schedule and group cooperation. "I want each one of you to tell us now what sort of piece you have planned, how many dancers you need, and when you plan to have your rehearsals. That way we can make sure that there are no scheduling conflicts in using the studio or sharing the same performers."

I am the only one who is doing a solo ballet piece. The others all have opted for modern work, mostly using five or six dancers. I'm grateful for their modern bent, for when I state that my piece will be set to text rather than music, no one bats an eye.

April 9

First day of rehearsal. You know how you picture and plan something over and over again in your mind—how it becomes more perfect with every plan, every thought? And then reality comes and shows you the true nature of ideas. Conception is a wondrous thing. Execution, however, can be another thing altogether.

I am torn between wanting to leave myself the freedom of improvisation and setting every move onstage. There are certain cues in the words (just as in music) that must always be the same, strictly choreographed. But the transitions keep changing on me.

I'm glad that Daria insisted that I have an advisor look over the project. Karol will see the piece for the first time next Friday. I want the movement to be clean by then. At least up to the rape scene. I've decided to use an umbrella, not only as a playful prop for the opening sequence, but as a phallic symbol. I want it always to be onstage, half open, pointing outward. This is very subtle, and I do not know if the audience will register it or not, but unconsciously it might seep into their brains.

April 11

This weekend was warm and sunny (a rarity), so Sam and I decided to go for a walk around campus and have a picnic. I took him to my favorite spot in Seattle, that special place on the cut of Lake Washington just below University Bridge.

We looked at all the sailboats together, and at the lovely, expensive houses, which sit on the opposite bank and stare back at us with windowpane eyes. Then we sat down on the freshly washed pontoon, my back resting against the top end of one of the large wooden pylons that keep the deck from floating away. Sam had his head in my lap and looked up at the sky while I read him my favorite of F. Scott Fitzgerald's Josephine stories, "Emotional Bankruptcy."

In this story, after years of flirting with boys from Princeton and Yale, stealing them away from other women for the sheer joy of conquest, the character Josephine finally falls in love with a soldier on his way to war. She knows that he is unlike other men, a man deserving of love, but when he offers her his hand, she realizes that she has played at love too long, has spent all real emotion on boys she never really cared about, and so has nothing left for him.

It is a marvelous tale, full of rich descriptions of fancy clothes and parties, with Fitzgerald's usual wistful nostalgia that always manages to stop just short of sentimentality. Without being moralistic, he manages to make us feel compassion for Josephine, while at the same time making us realize that her behavior would inevitably end in loss.

When I was done reading, Sam wanted to know why this was my favorite story.

"Because sometimes I feel like Josephine," I said.

"Do you fake love?" Sam asked.

"No, but so often I feel like I am faking everything else. Like in writing workshops you have to pretend that when people criticize your stories you don't take it personally. Or when you go to dinner with people whom you scarcely know, you have to eat whatever they put in front of you. I realize that it is only polite, but sometimes I get tired of doing the right thing, when the wrong thing often feels more comfortable."

I looked down at Sam's face. I noticed that his thick eyebrows form a "V" at the top of his nose. I kissed the spot where they meet.

"Does that sound terrible?" I asked.

"Someday I'm going to have a forty-five-foot ketch and sail it to Alaska," Sam said. "I'll call it *Bankruptcy.* People will see the name and think that I am a making a joke about how much the boat costs. But it will really mean that my boat will be a haven from the things that make you emotionally bankrupt."

I felt a lump in my throat. He understood.

"Can I come too?" I asked.

He didn't answer, but I felt his hands wrap more tightly about my waist.

APRIL 13 (Second Rehearsal)

The opening sequence is better, stronger. I think it is closer to what I want. Karol never showed up, so I began working on the rape section on my own. I think perhaps the text goes on too long before the actual rape occurs. I find myself randomly wandering around the stage just waiting for the moment the man catches Janie. He catches her metaphorically, of course—it is only Janie on the stage—the man is simply a voice-over, his harsh words pouring down upon her in torrents. But three minutes into the piece, I think the tension has already been created—no need to stretch out the climax much longer. Halfway through, the audience already expects something to happen.

Excitement stirs in me again. I have a long way to go with this piece, but I think it *can* work.

After rehearsal, I saw Daria. She said that I danced very nicely in ballet class yesterday. My heart soared. Such words make you feel humble, grateful, and secretly relieved. And just before I left, Daria touched me gently on the arm and her eyes went soft.

When a man touches me, there is excitement, pleasure, but I know the single touch will lead to another and another. It is sexual, a building desire. But with Daria and me, it is sensual, a different sort of desire, the desire for connection between two women. Will I ever be able to tell Daria of my love for her, or will that too remain a silent emotion inside me?

If only once in those four years at Mount Holyoke, she had cast me to perform in one of her pieces! After each audition, she would tell me "maybe next time," offering me hope like a canteen of water placed just out of arm's reach of a sun-parched man. She offered me hope, but never allowed me to actually drink from the canteen.

How is it that we can deeply love someone and hate him or her at the same time? Because by loving them, we give them power over us? By giving them that power, we are no longer their equal and thus begin to resent them.

APRIL 15

All my concentration is on *Ways of Being*. I think about it all the time. Walking to classes, at work, late at night, lying awake thinking. It seems completely real, the process, the story, the idea, while the world of classes and schoolwork and paying bills seems totally inconsequential.

I have become as obsessed with the process itself as I have with the piece. Perhaps because I know that I am recording it all for Eve or posterity or something like that. How does one go about creating a multimedia work?

In writing, straight writing, I worry about plot, continuity, always sure of my dialogue. But here I have no dialogue. Or I *do,* but it is the dialogue of the body and not the mind. I keep seeing the ideal over and over again in my head. And then remind myself of my personal limitations as a dancer and choreographer. I feel as though I am not expert enough to execute my own creation, as though my creativity is far more mature than my physical self.

I've decided on the lights. I want it stark, a woman exposed. Bright whites and violets. The rape scene redder and darker. I'm tormented about how to present the rape scene. I think about Santa Cruz, about what I am trying to do, and I worry that the audience will fail to understand. I want the audience to feel assaulted, just as Janie is assaulted.

Here they are in this nice theater, going out for an evening of dance, and someone has changed the rules. I want them to be angry at me for putting them through such an experience, and then for that anger to turn into comprehension. I know I can do this. I just have to keep thinking through the channels, making the dance tighter and tighter, clean it up so there are no doubts as to what I mean.

Like Janie, I find myself growing more and more removed from the world of speech and hearing. I give stock answers to questions, and grow annoyed when my thought processes are interrupted by the physical world. I keep up with schoolwork, but only because I know that when the piece is over I must return fully invested in the program.

Sam tries to support me, but he seems as unreal to me as the voices of my friends who call me every week on the phone from Boston. I feel like they are reading lines from a play and somehow I have walked in on the middle of it and have no idea what's going on. I am reading the lines of a different play.

APRIL 17

Today in class, Eve Porter talked about the experience of seeing a highway replace the open space where she had once taken her children to play. The implicit danger we feel when places of beauty and tranquility are replaced in the name of progress.

But I was born into a world that already knew the bomb. It is my legacy just as Nazi Germany is, McCarthyism, Vietnam, and the homeless on the street. I have never known a world different from this.

Eve asked, "What, as artists, do we owe?"

And suddenly I recalled a conversation I had with my mother when I was sixteen years old. She had just suggested to me that perhaps I should study social work when I went to college, or maybe dance therapy, so I could help others. I looked over at my mother, her face lined with fatigue and her thin brown hair starting to go gray. She had given most of her adult life to helping others, first as a teacher, then raising seven children, three of whom weren't even her own. I recalled how rarely my mother had time for private conversations with me about my life or career. I recalled her bitter outbursts that occurred far too often in my childhood, her raging about never having enough money or time for herself.

"I don't want to help the world," I told my mother. "I want to dance onstage."

And my mother said, "Shame on you."

I was sixteen years old and my mother said "shame." I had just told her the greatest secret of my life, my innermost hidden desire, something that until then I had never spoken aloud.

I have never forgotten the exchange, nor my mother's anger. I have never forgiven her for not understanding.

I have learned different lessons from those of my mother or Eve—that wars cannot be won, that Watergate was only the beginning of decades of political corruption, that Jews die, and Indians, and Blacks and anyone else who is different, that socialism fails to remain pure, and that democracy is not really about equality at all. I am not angry about these things (well, sometimes I am); I merely accept them.

I read somewhere that the best artists of an age come when an age is about to end. We haven't had too many good artists lately, so maybe we should take that as a positive sign. But it is an unjust world. And all of us, myself included, who worry far too much about being a successful artist than helping other people, are partly to blame for that injustice. But that is the way it is. It has always been that way. Only perhaps we are no longer afraid to recognize life for what it is. Contradictions. Half-truths. Bittersweet.

Life is red. Death is black. I am in love with both these colors. And I am never quite sure which I will choose. But somehow or other, despite myself, red continues to win out. Perhaps this is why I do not worry about the danger Eve talks about in class. Danger lies in the red zone. Danger lies with life. And danger is what makes me keep trying, that *frisson* of excitement, that moment when you hover at the brink, unsure if that day is the day you will fall over the edge.

And so I stop reading the newspapers and listening to the statistics and tune out the political debates. Instead, I use my eyes and look at the world before me. I walk the streets of the cities, of New York and Boston and Seattle, but more importantly, I walk the streets of myself and write about what I find there.

Eve Porter asked, "What do we owe?"

I ask, "What does the world owe us?"

And the answer for both is the same: merely life.

APRIL 18 (Third Rehearsal)

Karol still didn't show up to view the piece, so I worked on alone. The rape scene is definitely too long, so I changed it. Right now, however, I worry more about the transitions. They are not smooth enough. They do not register. A dance composition must be like a story. A dance phrase is like a sentence. And phrases must form paragraphs. And paragraphs must be linked to one another. *Ways of Being* is a narrative, just like any other kind of story, but as I am working against the literalness of words, seeking out the real truth, the physical truth as opposed to the subjective truth of words, it is crucial that each transition be precise. I think I need to slow down the movement a bit. I am pacing it too evenly. I've got to use the spoken text like music, with a rhythm and a time signature.

Three bloody toes today. The *pointe* shoes rip into my flesh, a painful reminder of how much work still needs to be done.

APRIL 19

I am in fragments. The pieces of my life are like pieces of a giant puzzle, each requiring my attention. Sam, and classes, trying to mail out stories for publication, and schoolwork, and my editing job, and dance classes, and Daria, and my friends back East. And *Ways of Being*. The title takes on import beyond its eight minutes. Eight minutes and months of my life. This happens whenever I work on a story. And each time I think to myself: "I am going crazy." And each time I think to myself: "What will it be like when it is finally done? Will I be any different? Will the emptiness inside me be filled at last?"

But this time I feel I'm spreading myself thinner than I have ever done before. I am taking a bigger risk this time. I am taking the two things that matter most to me, writing and dance, and laying them and my feelings about them before the world. It is a vulnerable place to be.

I am worrying too much. Worrying paralyzes me. It corrupts my work. I must be careful. To blow the fragile balance I have now would be fatal.

APRIL 21

Spent the day with my friend Marianne. We went to the Honey Bear, a neighborhood bakery-café near Greenlake. As we were ordering our tea and danish, I saw a large white-and-camel-colored collie pacing back and forth outside the entrance.

I recognized that dog. "Damn," I mutter under my breath.

"What is it?" Marianne says.

"That collie. His name is Percy. He belongs to Brad Baldwin. Brad Baldwin must be here."

We carefully scan the crowded room. Marianne finally spies him in the corner.

"I don't recognize the woman," Marianne says. "Is she in the English department?"

"That's Juleen," I say. "His girlfriend. The one he was still with when we dated."

"I can see you are not at all bitter about it," Marianne says, teasing.

"Not a bit," I say.

Marianne and I munch on our danish, thinking.

"You know what I don't get?" I say.

"What?"

"I'm involved with Sam now and he is twice the guy that Brad is. And if I was still involved with Brad, I never would have met Sam. So why does it still bother me?"

"Just because there is a new person in your life doesn't mean that the pain the other one caused you goes away."

"Let's go," I say.

"Do we walk past him?" Marianne asks. "Or go out the back?"

"Past him, of course," I say. "And make sure he sees us. And look really, really happy."

We walk by.

He doesn't wave or even acknowledge that he sees me. But I feel his eyes following my back as I walk right out the door.

When we get outside, I giggle with relief.

"Onward to better things," I say.

"To better things."

We go to Marianne's apartment, which she shares with her boyfriend, Marc. They are very happy together, which makes me relax and put Brad Baldwin away.

Marianne shows me some poems and journals she wrote when she spent her junior year in Germany. Instead of talking about the sights she saw, the people she met (including Marc), every entry records what food she ate that day.

"I was a bit bulimic in those days," Marianne says. "Food was the central preoccupation in my life."

I think about how during my senior year at Mount Holyoke I decided to live strictly on a diet of blueberry yogurt and Diet Coke. I thought if I could just lose five pounds, it would make me a better dancer. Unfortunately, the artificial sweetener in the soda gave me terrible stomachaches, which made it difficult to focus on my dancing.

"Women are so stupid," I say. "We are really, really stupid. And wonderful. And confusing."

Marianne also shows me the poems that some fourth-graders wrote. She is teaching at one of the public elementary schools as part of the university's poets-in-the-schools program. One of the poems is called "Peace" and is written by a ten-year-old girl. There is fear in the girl's poem. She makes reference to a secret that she cannot tell.

Peace is like a rabbit,
it is quiet, it is shy.
It will look you in the eyes
if you've been telling lies.
It tells you it will hurt you
like it did before if
you ever tell that sort of lie again.

I feel sick inside. I hand the poem back to Marianne quickly.

"What will you do?" I ask.

"I talked to her teacher," Marianne says. "There are no bruises. At least, none that we can see."

I ache for the little girl who writes about silence, about peace and silence being one and the same. Silence and lies. The little girl's name is Jennifer. Jennifer Virgin. A strange name for a little girl, one that is tinged with irony.

I keep picturing her face, a thin frail girl with big dark eyes.

Or perhaps that is too romantic. Perhaps she is a tomboy, dressed in blue jeans and carrying a rag doll in one arm and a stack of baseball cards in the back pocket of her jeans.

I want to write the story of a little girl named Jennifer Virgin.

I get home. Sam calls me up on the phone. I wait for his voice to comfort me, to wrap around me, to make me feel safe.

But his words fall flat, empty.

I am inconsolable.

April 22

Janie is everywhere. She pervades all aspects of my life, my alienation from my parents, my separateness from the external world; she's in Daria's grief for her dead father, and in the abused child in my new short story, "Telling Lies." She is everywhere but where she is supposed to be—onstage.

I feel her living inside me, yet she does not come to life in the ballet. I am too much aware that it is me dancing on the stage, not Janie. I have to let her fill my body, take over from the person who is busy worrying about her ego, about what her body looks like, if her feet are pointed enough, if Daria will be moved by *me,* not Janie.

How would Janie dance? She would not be dramatic. She would be chained to the ground, suppressed by all the voices that possess her, yet have that one element of defiance from which the new Janie, a free Janie, will be born.

How does Janie move?

April 23

Every few weeks in my novel-writing class, I submit a chapter of my book to be critiqued. The twelve of us sit around a large rectangular seminar table while Cecil Harris sits at the head. We go around in a circle, presenting our comments. The person whose work is being discussed is not allowed to speak until everyone has commented.

Listening to other people tell you what is wrong with your work is a torturous experience. The only thing that makes it bearable is that you know that the following week, you get to torture someone else. I totally despise the whole process, but as yet, I've never seen creative writing taught any other way.

Over the course of the quarter, I have heard many strange comments about my novel. "The kids are too intelligent for us to really like them," one person says. "Too many characters to keep track of.

Can't tell one from the other," another says to me. "Good descriptions, but nothing really happens. It's just too dark to be interesting."

Then it is Harris's turn to speak. He pauses.

"I've been thinking about this book," he says. "And I've decided that this whole manuscript is really about death."

A murmur goes about the room. Nods and affirmations. I sense that I am about to be welcomed into the magic circle like Jesus welcoming his disciples to the Passover Seder.

Harris looks over at me, making sure that I finally understand his observations.

"The opening scene takes place at a funeral," I say. "One character collects pictures of natural catastrophes. Another sleepwalks. Of course the book is about death and how people handle grief. It has been all along."

"Well, there it is," Harris says.

"Ah," everyone says.

I want to hit Cecil Harris, just as I suddenly know exactly why Judas thought Jesus a threat to the Jewish people. It was the disciples Judas feared, their sheeplike adulation, their worship of a person who probably didn't know any more than anyone else, but who just sounded more confident when he spoke. I want to hit Cecil Harris. I want to hit him as hard as I can.

April 25

Tonight, Sam, Marianne, and I went to see Adrienne Rich read at Kane Hall on campus. Originally, just Marianne and I were to go, but Sam said he had read some of Rich's early work in college and liked it.

I was both glad and amused, since Sam often makes negative, almost bitter comments about feminists and their supposed hatred of men. He makes comments like that often, which frightens me somewhat, but at the same time I often hear him speak admiringly of many of the early feminist writers and artists.

So the three of us went.

Rich was marvelous. She read from a new collection which explores more of her Jewish roots and also talks about the role she plays as mother to her sons. The tone of her poetry resonated within me far more than her actual words. A tone that conveyed both introspection and an embracing of the outside world.

Afterwards, as we all tried to exit from the overcrowded room, Marianne and I talked about how much we admire Rich. What it must be like to be that supremely talented, to still be growing and moving after thirty years of writing.

"She is so cool," Marianne said. "I'd give anything to meet with her just for five minutes."

"But you *can* meet her," Sam said. "The program notes said that there is a reception for her after the reading. It's just down the hall."

We looked at him aghast. After all, one couldn't just go up to a great poet unasked and talk with her.

Instead, Marianne and I decided to go use the restroom. When we got back to the lobby to meet Sam, he was nowhere to been seen.

"Great," Marianne said. "Where do you think he ran off to?"

"I have a good idea," I said.

We headed towards the room where the reception was being held. There hundreds of people, poets and would-be poets, were all making incredibly polite conversation. I hated it at once.

But in the center of the room, Adrienne Rich sat talking with some friends in a circle of chairs. "Oh my god," I said.

"What?" Marianne said.

"It's Sam."

Sure enough, Sam was down on his knees kneeling next to the great lady. She had her hand in his.

"I don't believe it," Marianne said.

I laughed.

When Sam spied us watching him, he excused himself from Adrienne Rich and came over to us.

"What did she say to you?" we asked.

"I told her I enjoyed the reading," he said, grinning. "She wanted to know what about it appealed to me as a man and a non-writer. She was very interested in knowing what I connected to."

"I don't believe it," Marianne said again.

"How did you even meet her?" I said. "This place is packed."

"Yeah," Sam said, "and everyone is just like you guys, afraid to talk with her, like she's some god or something. So, I just went over and introduced myself."

"Wow," I said.

"But that's not the best part," Sam said.

"There's more?"

"Before I went over to Adrienne, I was just standing around, sort of assessing the situation. This blonde chick comes over to me and starts chatting."

"She tried to pick you up?" I said. "At a feminist poetry reading?"

"Well, she wanted to know what I was doing there—me standing alone in my Huskies football jacket. She called me an oxymoron."

He grinned at me broadly.

"What?" Marianne said.

"I just taught Sam that term," I said. "We were talking about something or other and I said it was oxymoronic. Sam wanted to know what it meant."

"Yeah," Sam said. "A week ago I would have thought the woman had called me an idiot. You should have seen how disappointed she was when I mentioned that I had a girlfriend."

We all laughed.

"Listen," I said, taking Sam's arm as we walked out into the night towards the parking lot. "Do me a favor, will you? If Margaret Atwood ever comes to town, will you promise to come with me so that I can meet her?"

"Anytime you like," Sam said. "Who's Margaret Atwood?"

I didn't know whether to kiss him or throttle him.

APRIL 26 (Sixth Rehearsal)

Since Karol still hasn't shown up for any of my rehearsals, Daria has reluctantly agreed to serve as my advisor. Already, I can tell (with her help) that the piece is going better. I have reworked the end, the solo with piano music. This is crucial because the text ends there, and we finally hear the mute Janie speak through her movement. I use the theme of a circle, the definition of a face, and then expand it to encompass the whole body. Janie is dancing her circle dance and she re-encounters the umbrella/phallus. She wavers, unable to decide if she is strong enough to live within her own voice and not the voices of others. She reaches out to the umbrella as though to pick it up, but at the last moment she covers her face and draws the circle one last time.

Writing this journal makes me aware of how I create fiction and how I write this prose. When I write fiction, I hear the voices inside me, the dialogue of the different characters, the voice of the setting. Fiction, be it a story or a play or a dance, is the best part of me, the selfless me, the moment when I come out of myself and let the world come into me. When I write in this journal, I speak out loud as though having a conversation with myself. Journal writing is far more self-conscious and therefore not as true an art form. Here, I take myself far too seriously. I suppose I am compensating for being five foot four and weighing a hundred and ten pounds. People tend not to take you seriously when you look like that. People stare at the body, but rarely look at the soul.

I am fourteen. I am ninety-six. I have died and lived and died again. Janie is the product of one of my deaths.

April 28

This morning I told Sam that I loved him. I didn't even mean to say it, but it just slipped out. We've only been together a month. I don't even know if it's true, but it must be, for it was the only thing I could think of to say.

He kissed me after I said it. He said I was "special," which means nothing at all. He kept looking at his watch. He worried that his tea was getting too dark. Then he showered and dressed and dropped me back off here.

Just as I was about to leave his truck, he touched my arm and said, "I love you too."

I never should have said it. Once you say those words you can't take them back. The trap they put you in. You feel like your head is hanging in a noose and any moment they are going to open the floor below you.

But at least now maybe there will be somebody waiting below to catch me as I fall.

May 2 (Eighth Rehearsal)

Daria has finally seen the completed piece. She was very quiet afterwards.

I asked, "Is it boring?"

She said, "Not at all. I just didn't expect it. Right up to the time she was raped, I didn't expect it."

Then she said she perhaps wasn't the best one to help with this piece because she knew and loved my writing so much that she couldn't be completely objective. But she understood the point of the piece. What my aim was. So she can help me without changing its intent.

First thing she suggested was to cut all music entirely. The last section didn't add anything. She also said that to make the rape scene even more powerful, I should have it occur in complete silence. She objected to my use of the word "thing" in the voice-over narration. I suggested "penis."

She said they were both bad.

I said, "But rape is ugly."

She said, "But it will knock them dead, the silence."

She is right. Besides this *is* a piece about silence.

"But will the audience like it?" I asked.

"It will probably frighten them," she said.

MAY 6

I know about fear. Sometimes I think that is all I know. Fear of failure, fear of dogs, fear of earthquakes, fear of motherhood, fear of growing fat and old. Fear of not being good enough, never ever being good enough.

Tonight, however, I just suffered from basic old-fashioned stage fright. We had preliminary showings of each person's piece to determine the order of the program. I could not believe how nervous I was, just for a showing in the studio to other dancers. I haven't been nervous the whole time I rehearsed. But suddenly, in front of a small audience of twenty-five dancers, I balked. I realized the emotional impact of the piece. How personal it is. And I was scared. My legs shook on *pointe* the entire time.

Afterwards, there was polite applause. Nothing else. But Daria touched my leg, and said, "Yes. Yes. I like the changes you made." (I had quickly rechoreographed this morning before the showing, using her suggestions as a guideline.)

She said, "It is very powerful."

"But nobody said anything."

"They can't talk about it. It got to them. But I'll ask around later. See what the other faculty thought."

The six other pieces were all abstract. Some were quite beautiful. Some quite funny. But they all avoided anything sad.

Yet, later, after everyone had presented his or her work, Daria's assistant, an older woman with beautiful silver hair, came up to me. She said, "Are you okay? It is a very strong piece." And she hugged me.

I was still shaking. Somewhere between dance class and the showing, I had become Janie. I felt exposed like she did, vulnerable like she is... I felt the audience's stunned politeness cut through me.

MAY 8

Sam teases me because I insist my work is not political. He says: "I read your *Ways of Being* journal, don't tell me that's not political."

I said everything is political, but mine is personal politics, not national.

I do worry about that in terms of *Ways of Being*. I do not want people to misunderstand. I'm not trying to tell people rape is wrong; everyone knows it is wrong. To me, the piece is not about rape. Or if it is, it isn't so much about physical violation as it is about emotional violation.

When I told my kid sister Linda about the incident in Santa Cruz, about my incredible anger and weird sort of guilt, she said, "Yes, all women feel that way."

I said, "I am not all women. I am me. This has happened to me. Don't you dare turn this into a Cause." (She works for Greenpeace. She is very into fighting causes.) "I will not have myself turned into a statistic."

This is what the world has done to Janie, telling her to be a certain way, to represent a young American woman. Janie is not a representation. She *is* an American woman. She just happens to live inside of me.

MAY 11

Sometimes the most miraculous things happen in the most ordinary ways. After a heated debate with Eve Porter over whether content determines form or form determines content (I opted for the former), I decide to head over to the Creative Writing office to check my mail. Two weeks ago, I was turned down for a teaching assistantship for next year, so I have avoided my mailbox for several days, not wanting to get any more bad news.

And sure enough, there is that familiar manila envelope containing my manuscript and a form letter telling me that *The Seattle Review* had rejected yet another of my stories. I sigh and share the bad news with Anne Parsons, the woman who runs the office. She commiserates, but tells me that I shouldn't give up. She says you never know when you might get lucky.

There are fifty of us enrolled in the MFA program here (twenty-five in each year), plus dozens of undergraduate writers, so I have great respect for Anne, who, despite hearing the same complaints and fears from scores of students each day, manages always to sound like she cares about each one of us.

I ask her if Edgar Rutherford is in. I want to ask him to serve as my thesis advisor next year.

"Do you think he will do it?" I ask.

"You have to ask him," she says. "Let me make an appointment for you."

We make the appointment for the following Monday.

I bid Anne goodbye. I pull out the rest of the mail from my box, mostly flyers about upcoming readings by poets I have never heard of. There is also a white, unmarked envelope with my name on it. I walk down the halls of Padelford, reading.

It is a letter from the Milliman Prize committee. I have just won $5,000! The money is to be used to cover next year's tuition. Whatever cash remains after I make the payments belongs to me.

I run back to the Creative Writing office, waving the letter in the air. "I won," I tell Anne. "I won."

"I know," Anne smiles. "I put it in your box. I couldn't believe you didn't open it. You were so bummed out about the rejection letter from the *Review,* you didn't even bother to look at anything else. I wanted to burst out laughing."

"I won!" I said again.

"I told you not to give up," Anne says. "It is quite an honor, you know. To prevent favoritism among the faculty, we ask a board of editors and writers from around the country to select the winner. The committee told me that they felt your writing showed the most promise."

I hug her, then dance up and down the hallway of the English Department. Students and faculty walk by and stare at me strangely. I run back to the Creative Writing office yet again, taking deep breaths.

"I show promise!" I say.

Anne laughs with me.

It is everything I have dreamed about it. It is what I've worked for. I am grateful. I am happy.

Happy, happy, happy.

MAY 12

Sam and I celebrate by going out to dinner at a Chinese restaurant neither one of us can afford. I talk very fast and don't let him say a thing.

Later, I talk to Marianne over the phone. She tells me that she is very happy for me, but there is an edge to her voice that I haven't heard before. I suddenly remember she also had submitted her work for the Milliman Prize. Over fifty of us had applied. Only one could win.

"Oh, Marianne," I say. "I'm sorry. I shouldn't gloat."

"No. It's okay. Someone had to get it and I'm glad it's someone I like."

"I wish you could have won, too," I say.

"I'm still up for a couple of poetry prizes," Marianne says.

"You'll get one," I say. "I know you will."

But the conversation has brought me back down to earth. I am proud of myself, but now a nagging pit of guilt sits in my stomach. If Marianne had won and I had lost, would I have been as gracious?

In my heart, I know the answer. It is not a pleasant thing to know about yourself.

MAY 15

Awoke early. Before the alarm, which is unusual for me. Thinking about Janie and writing and Daria.

In rehearsal yesterday, it took three run-throughs before I rediscovered Janie in my body. The first run-through was Sandi, remembering the piece, the changes I made. It was too studied.

I find this fascinating... My immediate reaction in dance is to cling to technique, to keep the humanness out. It is only by running the piece again and again that I slowly transform steps into Janie's opening walk.

On Daria's suggestion I have created a story within the story, so that everything Janie does onstage has a particular purpose or narrative. Daria said most of the changes were dramatic improvements, but I could still go further with it. She said the *arabesques* still look too much like ballerina *arabesques*.

"What is Janie thinking about during that moment?" she asks.

"Being sixteen and being a ballerina."

"Has she studied?"

"No," I say.

"Then perhaps she can emulate one *arabesque* correctly; you know, from having watched dancers. But then on the second one, she perhaps looks around to see if anyone is watching her, and on the third one, the movement just feels so good she goes too far and ruins the line."

"Yes," I say. "That is why I choreographed the overdone Balanchine *arabesque*."

"Let us see her more self-conscious, then, let her want someone to notice her."

"You're asking me to bring back all my old dance habits," I say. "All the ones I've worked so hard to get rid of these past ten years."

Daria laughs, "So after June Fourth, you'll never do the piece again."

I laughed, too, but the word "never" ran through me with a shiver. I am going to be terribly sorry when Janie leaves me.

Live performance is not like a story you can read over and over again. After closing night, Janie will no longer exist. (On videotape, yes, but that is only the ghost of Janie.) I am going to miss Janie and the work I am learning from her.

After rehearsal, I sat in the hallway by Daria's office to take off my *pointe* shoes. Her office door was open, but she was looking out the window at the brick monolith. She didn't know I was there, but I watched her.

Very often I feel like a thief, stealing people's lives, observing them without their knowledge. Yet she is the most feeling person I know, so even if it is wrong to watch her in her private moments, I can't resist doing so. I know I watch her with longing, as if I were looking in the jewelry window at Tiffany's. I can win all the writing prizes in the world, but there still are things I cannot have.

MAY 22

Today is my twenty-fifth birthday. Sam gifted me with an electric-blue lace teddy from Victoria's Secret and a box of computer disks.

"For the both sides of you," he said.

MAY 26

Today, my story "Haymarket Station" appeared in *Art/Life* magazine. In lieu of payment, I received an author's copy in the mail. A red-letter day. For the first time my name is in print.

They spelled it wrong.

MAY 29

Edgar Rutherford calls me on the phone. We have been meeting fairly frequently over the past few months, and he always warmly encourages my work. However, it is unusual for him to phone me.

I ask him if something is wrong. (Typical of me, already in my head I've convinced myself that he is going to tell me that the Milliman Committee made a mistake and are giving the prize to someone else.)

"You're a friend of Felicia Phillips, aren't you?" Edgar asks.

"Sort of," I say. "She's just left for Australia. Why?"

"I just got the strangest call from her. She's in Sydney. Been there two days. Her husband, John, took off."

"What do you mean, took off?"

"Well, they arrived at the airport in Australia. Got through customs. Then John said he was going to get them a cab. He never came back. Felicia said he took all their savings with him."

"He abandoned her?" I say.

"Guess so. Anyway, she called me collect to ask if I could lend her some money."

"I'm sorry you got caught up in this, Edgar."

"She needed it. Of course I sent it."

"A lot of people wouldn't have. I mean, look at her own husband. If he was going to leave her, at least he should have done it before he abandoned her all alone in a strange country. So, you sent her the money to fly home?"

"No," Edgar says. "That's the strangest thing. She's going to stay. She met this couple through Traveler's Aid and they invited her to come live with them."

I feel my hands go cold. I'm not sure whether it is because I am floored by John's cruelty or at Felicia's audacity in calling a professor to ask for money. At her audacity and her incredible isolation that she must call a relative stranger for help rather than having a family member or even a close friend to turn to.

"She must be desperate," I say. "How horrible."

"Sounds like she could use a friend just now," Edgar said. "I don't really know who her friends are. Then I remembered that you came to her thesis defense last quarter. I thought you'd want to know. I got her address in case you wanted to write to her."

There is a strange sinking in my stomach.

I take the address.

"By the way," Edgar says. "I read the story you placed in my box. I thought it was terrific. The protagonist speaks with a true, thoughtful voice. If the rest of your work is that consistent, it will be delightful serving as your thesis advisor next year."

There is a lump in my throat.

"Thanks, Edgar. Thanks for everything."

I hang up the phone.

I dial Marianne Smithson's number.

"Hello?"

"It's me. Wait till you hear this..."

I tell her the story.

Marianne thinks we must write Felicia at once. Just to let her know that we care.

"But that's just it," I say, feeling terrible.

"What?"

"I never met anyone more tragic than Felicia," I say. "But I can't help feeling that she brings a lot of it on herself."

"She probably does," Marianne says.

"All Felicia Phillips wants is some recognition for her writing. And for someone to love her. So why do I despise her for not recognizing that John was a creep, when it was written all over him? Why do I despise her for all the terrible things that happen to her?"

"Because the strong part of you hates the weak part of you," Marianne says.

"There's that," I say.

"There's always that," Marianne says.

With a flash of pain, I think again of the sound of a pair of silver scissors cutting into a young Puerto Rican girl's dark silky hair at a summer camp in New Hampshire. I hate my own fear, and because I hate it, for years I have disowned not only the fear, but all those people, even those who needed my help, who reminded me of it.

I hang up the phone.

I turn on my computer.

After a few bleeps, I'm greeted by a blank screen and a blinking cursor.

The page is empty. Mine to do what I like with it.

"Dear Felicia..."

JUNE 1 (Dress Rehearsal)

We ran the piece twice because there were still problems with the light cues. As for myself, the hardest part is being able to become Janie from the very beginning of the piece. And I'm not going to get two chances on opening night.

Daria didn't say much—she just yelled at me because my *pointe* shoe ribbons were hanging out, looking sloppy. I must be sure to sew the ribbons down tomorrow and then stick them in place with hairspray (one of the dancers at the Joffrey Ballet taught me that years ago). A little later, though, Daria did tell me that I shouldn't worry about my technique—that I had plenty of technique to get me through the performance. It is one of the highest compliments she has ever paid me.

JUNE 2

Sam and I have had a fight. He called to say that he may not be able to make it to tonight's performance of *Ways of Being*.

"But you have to come see it," I said. "It's important to me."

"I have to work," Sam said. "You know I freelance. I work when I can."

"Can't you just tell them you have to leave early?" I said.

"Yeah, right. I'm going to tell them that they can't finish making their $100,000 commercial because I have to go see my girl-friend in a college dance concert."

"But you said that you would come. You promised."

"I have to work."

"Couldn't you have just said no?"

"If I say no, then maybe they won't call me the next time they need someone. I need the money. Besides, I saw the dress rehearsal."

"You care about your career more than you care about me."

Silence. I know we are treading on dangerous territory.

"Look, I'll try, okay? I'll try to get there in time."

"Don't do me any favors."

And I slam down the phone. My chest heaves with anger. I know I am being unfair. I also am terribly hurt.

All day I have been upset. I go over the conversation again and again in my mind. Part of me is right, I know it. But part of him is right, too.

I sit alone in my room all day and fume. I eat nothing. I shower and get ready to go to the theater.

At the theater, Daria gives company class onstage, an abbreviated *barre* and center that gets everyone warmed up quickly, but stops just before people begin to get too tired.

Daria wishes everyone good luck and says that those of us in the first act need to be dressed and ready to go on in thirty minutes.

All the performers dutifully follow each other down to the dressing room. I wash my sweaty face and wipe it dry with a freshly laundered towel. I do my makeup carefully, making sure that the pancake powder is spread evenly over my face and neck. I apply two different shades of eyeshadow, placing silver-white accents up along the outer rim and above the eyelids. Then I add a thick line of grease pencil underneath the lids and two coats of extra-rich mascara. I brush my cheeks with pink rouge and finish the picture with a bright red waterproof lipstick. If I wore such a face out in the street, people would think me a clown or perhaps a hooker. But from the stage, everything must be bigger and better than life.

I slip into my costume, a sleeveless teal unitard, carefully pinning my flesh-colored bra to the inside of the costume so it won't shift during the performance. I wish I could go braless, but Daria said that my breasts bounced just enough during dress rehearsal to be distracting.

I pull a sweater on over my unitard to keep me warm while I lace up my *pointe* shoes. I sew the end of the ribbons together so that they won't slip out. It creates a very clean line, but means that I must tie the shoes exactly right (too tight and I might get a cramp when I *relevé;* too loose and I won't have the support I need when I rise up on my toes), because once the ends are sewn together, I am basically stuck in the shoes until after the performance.

All this takes careful concentration, so I do not think about Sam at all. I don't think about anything except concentrating on the opening steps of the piece, those crucial first ten seconds when I have to convince the audience that I am Janie and beautiful and silent and scared simply by how I move.

I take the elevator back up to the theater. My piece is third, so I wait backstage until the stage manager calls my name. The piece before mine is a jazz work, light and frothy with lots of fun lifts and bright violet lights. I try to ignore the sound of the music coming from the stage, so it doesn't break my concentration.

"Waiting for the bus," I tell myself. "Janie, Janie is waiting for the bus…"

This is the opening sequence of the ballet. A young impatient Janie waiting for the bus to take her to school.

Even from backstage, I can hear the wave of applause for the dancers onstage. The sound of clapping makes my heart sing. It stirs me up; my pulse begins to pound a rhythmic joy.

"Block it out," I tell myself. "Waiting for the bus. Janie is waiting for the bus…"

Someone taps me on the shoulder. It is the stage manager, dressed all in black, a small clipboard in her hand. "You're up, Sandi," she whispers. "You're next."

I go out into the wings to wait for my cue.

The theater is dark as I take my place onstage.

The lights come up on me, a sole figure upstage left, dressed in a teal unitard and holding a matching teal umbrella.

Janie is waiting for the bus in the rain.

Janie loves the rain. She begins to dance in it, play in it.

It has begun.

When I get to the rape sequence, that strange painful sequence where a somewhat older Janie slides her hand down her groin and thigh and then holds her hand up into the light, showing it covered with imaginary blood and semen, I realize that there isn't a single sound in the audience.

They are dead quiet; not even a random cough disturbs the echoing darkness.

All eyes are on me. They are interested. They care.

I make the final gesture, Janie circling her face to lay claim to her own body.

Suddenly, it is over.

The applause doesn't come right away. Perhaps the audience isn't sure the dance is over, or maybe they are trying to decide whether it is appropriate to clap.

It doesn't come right away and I tense up.

It begins slowly from the back right corner of the theater. It begins slowly, then catches on. It is not thunderous; there isn't a large enough audience for thunder. Perhaps only 150 people.

But I hear it. It is real and loud, and as it rises to meet me on the stage, I feel a great release, an easing of a pain that has sat within me for so many months that I no longer even realized it was there.

The stage goes black.

"Congratulations," the stage manager says to me, as she hurries me off the stage. "Congratulations."

Then looking beyond to the group of dancers waiting in the wings, she says, "Next piece, please."

I am all alone. My body is slick with sweat. I know I should go back to the dressing room to shower and change, but I'm not yet ready. Instead, I take off my *pointe* shoes, throw them over my shoulder and, barefoot, climb the stairs back up to the studio.

I am alone with myself. Really alone, Janie gone, left down on that stage to meet the applause.

I am alone with myself and I enjoy it, feel it for what it is— to be alone and without pain.

"How'd it go?"

I turn around.

It is Daria.

It is Daria, dressed for once not in dance clothes, but in an elegant but simple suit. In her hand is an opened bottle of champagne.

"Didn't you see it?" I ask. "Weren't you out in the audience?"

She shakes her head.

"I was on my way downstairs when my assistant came in to tell me I had an important phone call. Everything was all set onstage, so I figured I'd take the call quickly, then come on down. Then someone brought in some champagne to celebrate opening night."

She holds the half-drunk bottle to me, "Do you want some?"

"Why not?" I say.

"Come to my office, then," Daria says. "I've got some glasses in my office."

I follow her numbly. Something is wrong. I know something is wrong. Daria would never miss opening night. After all, she is the artistic director.

We go into her tight tiny office. She pours me a paper cup of the golden champagne.

I take a sip, then wince as the liquor burns my throat. My body is warm from the performance, my stomach empty and taut.

"I probably shouldn't be drinking this," I say to Daria. "I haven't eaten a thing all day."

"Nerves?"

"No," I say. "I was just mad. Sam and I had a fight."

"But the piece went well?"

"I think so," I say. "I was hoping you'd tell me."

"I'm sure it was fine," Daria says. "You know my husband, Peter, saw dress rehearsal last week. He told me that artistically he thought your piece the most interesting."

"Are you telling me that I am good?" I ask, thinking that finally, finally she and I would come to the heart of it all.

"What did you and Sam fight about?" Daria asks suddenly.

"I told him that he thought his career was more important than mine. I mean, he makes lots of commercials. They're not even his—he just serves as the grip, and here it is my performance and he wasn't even sure if he could come."

Daria drank quickly from her glass.

"I know it's silly," I say. "Of course his career means more to him than mine does. I care about my career more than I do his. But I guess that's what scares me. In the past few weeks, I've often sacrificed writing time and sleep so that we could go out after he got off work. Sometimes, he will knock on my window at three in the morning. He doesn't want to wake my suitemates, so he doesn't ring the bell. He just knocks on my window until I wake up. Then we go to the College Inn. He has dinner. I have breakfast."

"Sounds nice," Daria says.

"It is. Sort of like *Sleeping Beauty* or something, the hero coming to wake the heroine. I guess I am just questioning if it is possible to be a great artist and have a good relationship at the same time. I shouldn't be involved with him. I should be writing everyday. At least until I get my career really going."

"Peter's leaving," Daria says suddenly. "You know he's a painter. He only moved to Seattle to be with me. He just can't seem to find a place to show his work here. He says I care more about my dancers than I do him. Maybe I do."

"Oh," I say.

"Anyway, we've been fighting about it a lot. It's gotten so bad that lately I've just been sleeping on the floor instead of going home."

"Here? You sleep on the floor of your office?" I say.

I think of my beautiful Daria sleeping on a dirty carpet in a tiny, closed-in room. I am miserable. I feel powerless to help her. I know nothing about coping with adult relationships. I've kept them away, first by dating married men, then by having that silly obsession with Brad. Now with Sam there is nothing to keep us apart. Nothing except my own fear that loving someone else means giving up something of myself. Nothing except this most important foolish fight that we had. Now I'm not sure if I'll ever see him again.

"Maybe he'll change his mind," I say, helping myself to a second glass of champagne, wondering if I am talking about Peter or Sam.

"The call I mentioned earlier," Daria says. "That was him. From the airport. He said he really hated to wreck my opening night, but since I hadn't been home in three days, he thought I might like to know."

"Oh, Daria," I say and want to embrace her.

But she is sitting behind her desk on a hardback swivel chair, boxed in by the radiator on one side of the room and the file cabinet on the other. By the window, a bunch of leftover costumes are piled up on a chair, temporarily obscuring the view outside. To reach her, I would have to climb over the desk, messy with the stacks of paperwork that a department chair must wade through every day.

But it is only when I notice a few throw pillows on the floor that I really understand how inaccessible she really is. Not only to me, but perhaps to herself as well. She would rather sleep here than confront a troubled marriage. She would rather sleep here than call a friend for a good cry and a night's stay on a living-room couch.

Such knowledge should make me feel strong. It does not. It makes me weak with pain. It makes me weak with pain to know that the person I most respect in the world is as vulnerable and as confused as I am.

As I am about to pour myself yet another glass of champagne, Daria reaches her arm across the desk and gently squeezes my bare foot, which is resting on the ice cold radiator.

"You should put something on," she says. "Then we will go down and see the end of the concert."

And she hands me a pair of slippers and one of her oversized sweatshirts that is hanging on the back of her door.

I put them on.

We take the elevator back down to the lobby of the theater. The concert is nearly over. From behind the closed doors, we hear the audience applauding the last piece. The applause goes on for a long time.

Then, suddenly, the theater doors open and the crowd begins to pour out of the exit with the force of a tidal wave. In a second, Daria is totally surrounded by people, by the parents of students, by faculty, by would-be and former dancers, by balletomanes.

As the crowd continues filling up the lobby, I am swept away from Daria, swept away from the crowd in general, until my back is pressed flat against a wall in the corner of the room.

And then I see him. Sam. His six-foot-three-inch frame towering above everyone else.

"I love you," he mouths to me from across the room.

"I'm drunk," I mouth back.

He frowns, not understanding.

"What?"

"I'm drunk," I say, when he is at last beside me. "I'm really, really drunk."

He envelops me in his embrace.

ABOUT THE AUTHOR

A graduate of Mount Holyoke College, Sandi Sonnenfeld holds an MFA in creative writing from the University of Washington, where she was recipient of the Loren D. Milliman Scholarship. Her short stories, essays, and journalism pieces have appeared in a wide variety of publications, including *Harvard Business Review, Wall Street Journal's National Business Employment Weekly, Animals, Transitions Abroad, Sojourner, ACM, Raven Chronicles, Voices West,* and *Hayden's Ferry Review,* as well as in three anthologies. A member of PEN Center West and the Society of Professional Journalists, Sandi lives in Seattle. *This Is How I Speak* is her first book.